D1565762

SPECIAL FORCES/RANGER-UDT/SEAL
HAND-TO-HAND COMBAT/SPECIAL WEAPONS/
SPECIAL TACTICS SERIES

KNIFE FIGHTING,
KNIFE THROWING FOR COMBAT

SPECIAL FORCES/RANGER-UDT/SEAL HAND-TO-HAND COMBAT/ SPECIAL WEAPONS/ SPECIAL TACTICS SERIES

KNIFE FIGHTING, KNIFE THROWING FOR COMBAT

by Michael D. Echanis

Transcribed by N.M. Killian

BLACK BELT BOOKS
A Division of **OHARA ⓟ PUBLICATIONS, INC.**
World Leader in Martial Arts Publications

Thirteenth printing 2005
ISBN-0-89750-058-X

PUBLISHER'S NOTE

This book is the second in a series of basic reference texts dealing with hand-to-hand combat/special weapons training and tactics for the Special Warfare Branches of the United States Military. It is intended for use by Airborne/Rangers/Special Forces/UDT/SEAL/ Force Recon/Commando personnel.

Subsequent volumes will follow, bringing a series of texts dealing with all aspects of the newest form of close-combat warfare developed for Special Warfare units since 1942. This system of training was developed from the basis of an ancient system of fighting, HWARANGDO, utilized by Korean warriors for over 2,000 years, reconstructed and developed for use by a Special Research Group comprised of former Special Forces/Rangers/UDT/SEAL Instructors for hand-to-hand combat, headed and directed by Mr. Echanis.

DEDICATION

"The credit belongs to the man who is actually in the arena, whose face is marred by dust and sweat and blood . . . who knows the great enthusiasm, the great devotions; who spends himself at a worthy cause; who at best knows in the end the triumph of high achievement, and . . . if he fails, at least fails daring greatly so that his place shall never be with those cold, timid souls who know neither victory nor defeat."

—John Fitzgerald Kennedy

This book is dedicated to His Excellency, the Honorable President of Nicaragua, General Anastasio Somoza Debalye, and to his son, Major Somoza, and to their endless cause and struggle of combating the spread of communism through the utilization of terrorism and subversion in this free world.

PUBLISHER'S FORWARD

For over 2,000 years, HWARANGDO has been a major, but little-known, Korean martial art. It emerged from the shrouds of secrecy only within the past few years. For centuries HWARANG-DO served as a model system and institution of study for a core of young aristocrats who would later produce the generals, statesmen and great leaders of Korea.

Certain units of the Special Warfare branches of the United States Military have incorporated HWARANGDO into their own training. To do this, they have had to immerse themselves completely into that ancient martial art.

For the first time, the ancient ideals and systems of combat are brought into the contemporary American military training experience. A portion of this training has provided the basis for this book. We cannot stress enough that it is a *basic text only*.

SPECIAL FORCES/RANGER-UDT/SEAL HAND-TO-HAND COMBAT/SPECIAL WEAPONS/SPECIAL TACTICS SERIES, *Knife Fighting, Knife Throwing for Combat*, marks a milestone in military and martial arts publications.

Ohara Publications

ABOUT THE AUTHOR

MICHAEL D. ECHANIS is the developer and former Senior Instructor for the Special Forces/Ranger Hand-to-Hand Combat/ Special Weapons School for instructors and the former Senior Instructor for the UDT-21, SEAL-2 Hand-to-Hand Combat/Special Weapons School for instructors. He has given seminars, demonstrations and advanced training to unconventional warfare experts from all over the world. His system of training has been termed by BLACK BELT magazine as "one of the most effective systems of hand-to-hand combat in the modern world." *Soldier of Fortune* magazine has termed him as "one of the leading experts in hand-to-hand combat in the world today."

Mr. Echanis is a former Special Forces Ranger and is privately tutored by Joo Bang Lee, the Supreme Grand Master of hwarangdo. He specializes in Un Shin Bup, the art of invisibility, the Korean counterpart to Japanese Ninjitsu and termed for modern military use as sentry stalking, silent killing. He is the first American Sul Sa in the history of Korean martial arts.

Mr. Echanis is currently studying the advanced mental aspects of hwarangdo that apply to ki, internal energy. He has demonstrated his ability to utilize and control the five types of mental, physical power utilized in combat by hwarangdo warriors for over 2,000 years. Similar to the ancient testings of North American Indian warriors, hwarang warriors equally test themselves in breaking the barrier of changing from man to warrior.

Mr. Echanis has pierced the flesh of his neck and arms with needles while suspending buckets of water, demonstrating no pain or bleeding. He has had cars and military vehicles driven over his body while in a prone position. He has demonstrated the ability to make his body immovable so that 100 soldiers could not lift or move him. He seemingly turns his body to steel as cement is crushed upon his chest while he is lying on a bed of nails or while receiving focused blows to vital portions of the body as demonstrated by holding an ax blade to the throat and other portions of the body and receiving full-focused blows with a 2"-x-4" to the edge of the blade. The fifth, perhaps the most difficult to attain, is controlling this power directly with your mind and directing it to individual parts of the body and finally extending it outside the physical body through thought in conjunction with a special breathing technique. Mr. Echanis has demonstrated this technique and utilizes it in the study of Kookup Hwal Bub, the study of acupressure and acupuncture as utilized to revive an injured person during combat.

Mr. Echanis has studied the advanced portions of Chuem Yan Sul, the ancient study of Buddhist priests in the ability to focus the mind through concentration, sometimes termed as hypnosis.

Mr. Echanis heads a Special Research Group of former Special Forces Rangers and UDT/SEAL Hand-to-Hand Combat experts who have developed a new system and approach to teaching, as directed by the guidelines of military instruction. Using the 2,000-year-old index of knowledge and battlefield experience utilized by hwarang warriors of Korea, this system of hand-to-hand combat/special weapons and special tactics has been tested and evaluated by unconventional warfare experts all over the world and the quality and professionalism of the program and its instruction is a reflection of Mr. Echanis himself.

Ohara Publications

HWARANGDO
ITS KOREAN HISTORY AND INTRODUCTION TO AMERICA

The present nation of Korea was once divided into three kingdoms. They were Koguryu, Paekche and Silla. Koguryu was the largest, at least in the beginning. It occupied the entire territory of present-day Manchuria as well as the northern part of the Korean peninsula.

In the fifth century, Koguryu made a bid to take over its two smaller neighbors. Paekche was almost overrun and forced to move its capital southward. Silla was constantly harassed. But here an unusual phenomenon was taking place that would one day make Silla the leading Korean kingdom.

Silla didn't break under the military pressure of Koguryu. Rather, the kingdom united and created new institutions to make it a formidable fighting machine. Foremost among the new institutions was the Hwarang. It included a core of young men of nobility who would produce the generals, statesmen and other leaders.

The great period of the united Silla was from 661—935 A.D. It was a time of immense development. Says martial arts historian Sang Kyu Shim, "The Hwarang entered a monumental period of peace, prosperity and development, inventing movable type 200 years before Gutenberg. It [Silla] also became a profoundly Buddhist country, printing lengthy Buddhist scriptures and constructing countless Buddhist temples and sculptures throughout the country."

Prior to 57 B.C., in the peninsula now known as Korea, a group called Won Hwa, a group of women, met for philosophical and intellectual discussions. This group was the ancient forerunner of hwarangdo.

At the time when Silla was being threatened by its larger and stronger neighbor, Koguryu, the people and government of Silla organized under the leadership of the Supreme Buddhist Monk Won Kwang Bopsa, a school of intellectual pursuits and martial arts thinking. This school came to be known as the Hwarang, or "Flower of Manhood." To this temple school, the king of Silla sent his sons and trusted soldiers to be trained in the philosophical codes and martial arts techniques developed by Won Kwang Bopsa.

Because of the martial arts training and particularly the philosophical and moral codes taught by the founders of the hwarangdo system, the tiny country of Silla eventually overcame the strength and size of its neighbors, Paekche and Koguryu, and ruled the peninsula known as Korea for many centuries.

Two of the Hwarang warriors, Kui San and Chu Hwang, were

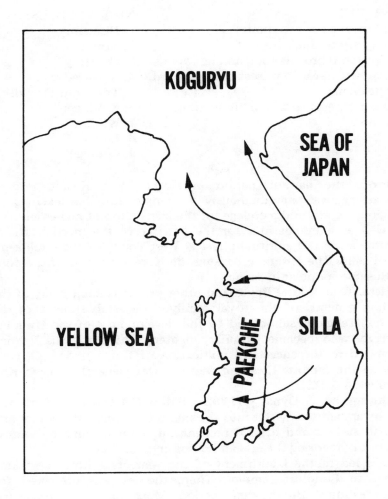

instrumental in obtaining from Won Kwang Bopsa a set of five rules by which they could govern their lives and purify their minds. Adding these rules to the virtues practiced by hwarangdo students already, the warriors had an all-encompassing set of guidelines by which they could conduct themselves properly as martial artists and as human beings. This set of guidelines is still remembered and practiced today by students of hwarangdo:

FIVE RULES:
1. Loyalty to one's country.
2. Loyalty to one's parents.
3. Trust and brotherhood among friends.
4. Courage never to retreat in the face of the enemy.
5. Justice never to take a life without cause.

NINE VIRTUES:
1. Humanity
2. Honor
3. Courtesy
4. Knowledge
5. Trust and Friendship
6. Kindness
7. Wisdom
8. Loyalty
9. Courage

From the earliest period in Korea, Won Kwang Bopsa's monastery was simultaneously a temple for the teaching of religious beliefs and a college for the instruction of higher learning as well as a gymnasium for the practice of the martial arts. It became a kind of spiritual/physical West Point for the intelligentsia of Silla. The Hwarang became the Korean version of the code of Bushido, popular in Japan.

Here, Won Kwang Bopsa and other priests trained many of the leading generals of the royal family. The establishment of the military/religious school led to the development of the Hwarang warriors who became legendary fighters. This ferocious fighting spirit led to the successful unification of Korea under Sill rule. Among the famous Hwarang warriors was General Yoo Sin Kim (595—673 A.D.).

During the Yi Dynasty (1392—1910 A.D.), the martial arts and the hwarangdo code fell into decline. The purely intellectual arts rose in stature and official recognition. With it came a dynastic policy of "favoring the arts and despising arms."

This led to the banishment of the warriors, with some taking refuge in Buddhist temples. There the art was preserved for centuries until the modern period. Much like the monks and monasteries were centers of learning during the so-called European Dark Ages, the Buddhist monks and temples in Korea preserved what they could of both the physical and religious aspects of hwarangdo.

Hwarangdo remained in Korean temples until the early 1950s. At that time, two Korean brothers, Joo Bang and Joo Sang Lee, began to study the art. They would soon bring it to the Korean population and later, America.

The Lee brothers were born in the 1930s. Their father was a martial artist, having black belts in judo and kendo, the only martial arts available under the Japanese Occupation. Father Lee began the boys' martial arts training early, training them at home as early as the age of two years old.

At the age of five, Joo Bang and Joo Sang were enrolled in the So Gwang Sa Buddhist Temple for religious and martial arts training, this temple being the current residence of the Grand Master of hwarangdo, a monk named Suahm Dosa.

In 1950, the Lee family moved to the southern tip of Korea, and the boys were enrolled in the Yang Mi Ahm temple on O Dae Mountain, where Suahm Dosa had also relocated. The Lee brothers' training continued here, and in 1960, they received permission from their master to open a hwarangdo school in public, the first one in modern times, in Seoul, Korea. Subsequent to the opening of the first school in Seoul, the Korea Hwarang-Do Federation was granted a government permit to function as a martial arts association in Korea.

In 1968, Joo Bang Lee was presented with the Lion's Award as the Martial Artist of the Year. 1968 was also the year hwarangdo first came to the Western world. In that year, Master Joo Sang Lee came to the United States and opened a hwarangdo school in Huntington Park, California.

In 1969, Master Suahm Dosa died and the position of Grand Master was passed to Joo Bang Lee. This position made Joo Bang Lee the Grand Master of hwarangdo in an unbroken line of succession lasting over 1,800 years, directly descending from the two warriors and hwarangdo masters of Won Kwang Bopsa's time, Kui San and Chu Hwang. In 1972, Joo Bang Lee came to the United States to spread the art of hwarangdo. Today, there are approximately 56 hwarangdo schools in Korea and another 38 in the United States and Europe. Joo Bang Lee is the Grand Master of hwarangdo and President of the International Hwarang-Do Federation, and his brother Joo Sang Lee is the Head Master and Chairman of the International Hwarang-Do Federation.

HWA RANG DO

花郎道

THE GRAND MASTER OF HWARANGDO
JOO BANG LEE

道主 李柱邦

Mr. Echanis is privately tutored by the Grand Master of Hwarang-do, Joo Bang Lee, in the secret portions of the inner arts.

SPECIAL OPERATIONS,
RESEARCH AND DEVELOPMENT GROUP
SENIOR ADVISORS AND HEAD INSTRUCTORS
OFFICE FOR THE STUDY OF CONFLICT AND TACTICS

SENIOR ADVISOR NAVY/SPECIAL WARFARE STUDIES

    MASTER CHIEF PETTY OFFICER NISSLEY/
    U.S. NAVAL ADVISOR USAJFKCENMA
    UNITED STATES NAVY

SENIOR ADVISOR ARMY SPECIAL WARFARE STUDIES

    MASTER SERGEANT
    JAKOVENKO/5TH SPECIAL FORCES GROUP
    UNITED STATES ARMY

SENIOR ADVISOR PSYCHO-PHYSICAL STUDIES

    MASTER SERGEANT
    JACKSON/HEAD INSTRUCTOR
    SPECIAL FORCES MEDICAL SCHOOL
    FORMER VIETNAM P.O.W.

HEAD INSTRUCTOR

    SPECIAL FORCES/HAND-TO-HAND COMBAT
    SPECIAL WEAPONS INSTRUCTORS' TEAM
    SERGEANT SANDERS/5TH SPECIAL FORCES GROUP
    UNITED STATES ARMY

HEAD INSTRUCTOR

    82ND AIRBORNE RAIDER RECONDO/HAND-TO-HAND COMBAT
    SPECIAL WEAPONS INSTRUCTORS' TEAM
    STAFF SERGEANT O'NEAL, RANGER INSTRUCTOR
    UNITED STATES ARMY

HEAD INSTRUCTOR

    UDT-SEAL/HAND-TO-HAND COMBAT
    SPECIAL WEAPONS INSTRUCTORS' TEAM
    1ST CLASS PETTY OFFICER PAAINA
    SEAL TEAM II
    UNITED STATES NAVY

HEAD INSTRUCTOR

    FORCE RECON/HAND-TO-HAND COMBAT
    SPECIAL WEAPONS INSTRUCTORS' TEAM
    STAFF SERGEANT O'GRADY
    2 FORCE RECON UNITED STATES MARINE CORPS

HWARANGDO
AND ITS RELATIONSHIP TO HAND-TO-HAND COMBAT

Hand-to-hand combat is as old as the human race. Fighting techniques developed as warfare became more organized, and the different fighting styles which evolved were modified and influenced by the different cultures and traditions of the period. But only in Asia did different styles of empty-handed combat become an art regarded as secrets of the State or harbored within the walls of the religious monasteries. The Asian fighting arts were frequently connected with religious movements of Buddhism. Within the Buddhist religion there were both a fighting and a pacifist sect.

Hwarangdo differs from many other of the more familiar martial arts in that it is designed purely as a way of deadly fighting. It is not intended to be an educational system, a competitive sport, a form of self-improvement, although it can be all these things. Consistent with its origins as a fighting system for feudal warriors, hwarangdo includes all forms of personal combat, as well as training in the use of hand weapons and instruction in revival techniques. Its advanced stages encompass the occult mental disciplines of the inner arts.

Hwarangdo does not fall either into the hard, linear category of martial art, or into the soft, circular category. Rather, it includes both hard and soft, both straight-line and circular. Hwarangdo is considered a dialectical form of combat, inasmuch as it contains opposite or contradictory elements within its single unity, and derives its strength from the dynamic interbalance between the two. This dialectical conception flows from Asian cosmology, symbolized by the swirling circle in the South Korean flag, which holds that all opposing forces of the universe, uhm and yang in Korean (yin and yang in Chinese), are indivisible.

Hard and Soft Styles

Uhm symbolizes softness and darkness, and is represented in the martial arts in the soft fighting styles. Its power is that of gently flowing water that changes the shape of stone. Its typical motion is circular, with the force of a whip, or a rock whirled on a string, and its tendency is to unite and combine to close in.

Yang symbolizes hardness and brightness, and is represented·in the arts in the hard, linear forms of fighting. Its strength is that of steel or rock, and its typical motion is straight lines and angles, with force derived from leverage. Its tendency is to maintain distance between opponents.

Hwarangdo incorporates the elements of uhm along with the elements of yang. Its karate-like techniques involve straight punches and kicks of the familiar type, but they also include spectacular circular spin-kicks, some traveling as much as 540 degrees before impact, a build-up of tremendous centrifugal force. These kicks can be aimed at the body or at the head, or they can whip in at mat level to cut an opponent's feet out from under him.

A punch or a kick from an opponent, or a blow from a weapon, may be met in kind, or it can be answered with a breaking of joints, a throw, or an attack against the opponent's nerves or acupuncture points. It can be met with a hard block and finished with a punch or a kick, or it can be met with a loose-wristed deflection similar to the Hawaiian lima-lama techniques, trapped by the flexible hand, and finished with a throw or a joint-dislocation.

Hwarangdo includes a complete discipline of throwing techniques, some similar to the body throws of judo, others similar to the pain throws of aikido. But hwarangdo throws are always executed in their combat, or disabling form, never in their sport form.

Hwarangdo training also includes counter-throws, finger-pressure techniques (more than 300) applied against nerve or acupuncture points, 30 different choking techniques and a system of ground fighting or matwork based to some extent on ancient Mongolian grappling.

Weapons training includes kumdo (Korean kendo), both with the bamboo sword and with the live blade, stick-fighting with all lengths of sticks, short-sword and spear techniques, knife throwing and the throwing of dirks, pointed stars, stones, etcetera.

At advanced black belt levels, students begin to learn the healing arts of acupuncture and finger-pressure revival.

When hwarangdo students reach fourth-degree black belt, they may qualify for training in a martial art completely different from the techniques they have learned before, consisting of 36 categories of killing techniques.

HWARANGDO'S DYNAMIC TECHNIQUES

Hwarangdo techniques are founded on three basic divisions of power—inner, exterior and mental. Aspects of each are taught as the student progresses in his training. Hwarangdo includes all forms of personal combat. It is a true yin/yang martial art. Both hard/soft and straight-line/circular forms and techniques are found in hwarangdo.

In advanced studies, hwarangdo deals with mental disciplines and becomes an "inner art." The techniques and principles are effective for such diverse needs as personal self-defense, mob control and mental discipline.

On the purely physical and technical level, the knowledgeable practitioner will spot forms similar to a broad range of martial arts. Below is a breakdown of the techniques in which hwarangdo students are instructed:

A. INNER POWER TECHNIQUES (NEGONG):

These are developed by controlled breathing and concentrating or focusing the ki at a single point. It is said to be the essence of power behind kicking and punching. The techniques are broken down in 21 subdivisions:

1. Joint techniques. These are self-defense techniques directed at the opponent's joints.

2. Throwing techniques.

3. Breathing exercises. These are learned in order to develop power by breath control.

4. Head techniques. These encompass techniques for using the head as a weapon.

5. Hand-breaking techniques. These include self-defense movements *against* hand grabs.

6. Kicking techniques. These are based on three basic kicking types: snapping, thrust and circular.

7. Finger-pressure techniques.

8. Choking techniques.

9. Rolling techniques.

10. Self-defense techniques from a seated position.

11. Self-defense techniques from a prone position.

12. Punching and striking techniques.

13. Forms. There are 30 forms or *hyung*, patterns or series of movements used as training forms so that the student can learn techniques.

14. Breaking boards or stones. These techniques stem from the combination of physical and mental power or outer and inner strength concentrated at a single point.

15. Tearing of flesh with bare hands.

16. Unarmed self-defense against knife attack.

17. Counter-defense against throwing techniques.

18. Counter-defense against kicking attacks.

19. Counter-defense against punching attacks.

20. Come-along or hand control techniques.

21. Defense against more than two opponents.

B. EXTERIOR POWER TECHNIQUES (WAY-GONG):

This section of instruction deals with what is commonly known in kung fu or karate as weapons training. Hwarangdo students learn the use of the sword, stick, spear, short sword, knife and other exotic weapons, such as throwing dirks, pointed stars and stones.

C. MENTAL POWER TECHNIQUES (SHIN-GONG):

These techniques directly affect the "life energy force" of the human body. They are divided into six areas:

1. **KIAPSUL.** Here a combination of physical, mental and breathing power plus concentration

is learned in order to break solid objects more efficiently.

2. **KYUK PA SUL.** Extracting mind power. Refers to the capacity of the mind to extract latent power inherent in every human. The mind may possess a 100-percent potential, but the normal condition is a person who uses only a small portion of this power. It is possible with the proper training, according to the Lee brothers, to develop the full potential.

3. **CHUEM YAN SUL.** Technique of putting a person to sleep.

4. **KOOKUP HWAL BUB.** Use of acupuncture to revive an injured person.

5. **CHIMGOO SUL PUP.** Acupuncture as a medicinal science.

6. **GUN SHIN PUP.** The art of concealing oneself in front of others. It employs a combination of distraction, suggestion, stealth and camouflage used by spies and assassins, such as the celebrated Japanese Ninja.

THE THEORY OF KI POWER IN HWARANGDO

Grand Master Joo Bang Lee explains the theory surrounding ki power in this way. The *danjun* area, or seat of this power in the human body is located one to three inches below the navel. It is comprised of three points: *ki hae*, located one inch below the navel; *kwan won*, two inches below, and *suk mon*, three inches below the navel.

This danjun is the center from which all life energy, or power, emanates. Lee says that a human being cannot even move one finger without the power from danjun. Although all people have this power, not everyone has the same level of control over it. But with the proper training in special techniques devised and developed by hwarangdo masters over the last 2,000 years, it is possible to increase the level of ki power over which a person has control.

This ki power in hwarangdo functions in five different ways. One way is to make the body heavy. Another is to make the body light. The third is to make the body feel like steel. The fourth is to make the body numb, so that no pain is felt. The fifth, and perhaps the most difficult to attain, is to control this power directly with your mind in individual parts of the body and even outside the physical body. An example of this last form of ki power would be to use the power to make your arm or leg move faster than is possible by purely physical means, as in the execution of a punch or kick.

In American schools, students are taught to develop ki power through the following two basic methods:

1. Danjun ki (air ki): The scientific application of controlled breathing techniques to build up ki power.

2. Shin ki (mental ki): The use of mental techniques taught through meditation to gain mastery over unlimited amounts of ki power purely through the medium of mind control. Examples of this method occurring spontaneously without prior training are the many documented cases of persons who, under extreme fear or stress circumstances, lift or move an object which would normally require the strength of ten people, such as a mother lifting a car under which her child is trapped.

Hwarangdo ki theory also delves into the study of what is said to be the movement in and out of the body of the "spirit" or "life force," particularly that movement which occurs near or at the time of death. In the region of the eighth to tenth vertebrae (from the top of the spine), hwarangdo masters explain, is a "door," or exit point, where the spirit leaves the body at the time of death. This door is called *myung mon sa hwa hyel.*

The importance of ki theory is relevant to a basic tenet of hwarangdo training—the belief that the martial artist must be able to heal injuries and illness because he has the power to cause them. Therefore, students undergo medical training (acupuncture, herbal medicine, bone setting, etcetera), prior to learning the more dangerous and deadly black belt techniques.

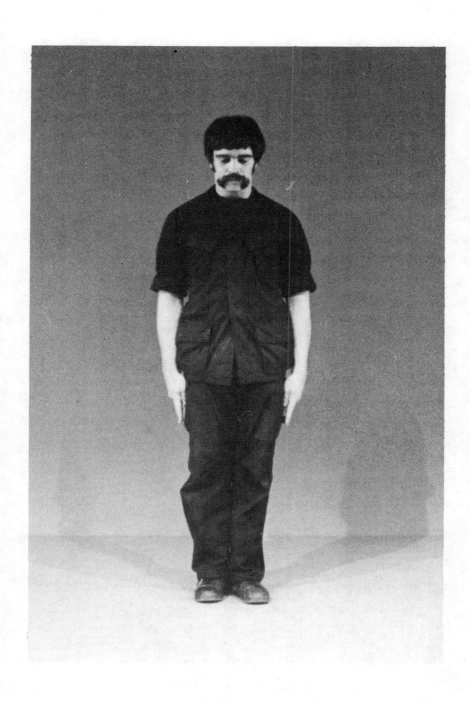

Part I
KNIFE FIGHTING FOR COMBAT

INTRODUCTION

The knife has been utilized during hand-to-hand combat for thousands of years. Since the day the knife was created, it has served a dual purpose, as a tool for survival and a weapon for combat.

Considered a maiming or killing tool, the knife presents a terrifying, psychological effect in the eyes of the enemy. Once the knife becomes a combat weapon, utilized in the hands of a well-trained, professional soldier, it automatically injects a deadly lethality to his capabilities, integral to his survival and to the accomplishment of his mission. The knife serves as a multipurpose weapon for the combat soldier of today. Utilizing it as a method of lethal close-quarter combat and as a tool for survival, it becomes an integral piece to the combat soldier's everyday equipment.

Proficiency in the use of the knife as a combat weapon brings the individual soldier to a true sense of security, having the confidence to encounter and defend against much larger assailants and to control and eliminate multiple attackers due to the lethality of the knife as a weapon in hand-to-hand combat. The knife provides a third vehicle of use for the soldier in the aspect of free-form practice of simulated attacks.

The practice movements of the training exercise utilized by the knife trainee can be used as methods of maintaining mental alertness and increased focus of attention, seeming to clear the mind and bring about a better ability to comprehend and retain at an increased level of mental input. Knife training can be a great asset during periods of confinement or isolation, such as being entirely alone while conducting operations for extended periods of time behind enemy lines during survival; or as a prisoner of war in confinement, giving availability to physical exercise and development in conjunction with increased mental awareness instilled from physical fitness and a mental sense of well-being. Men such as Pappillon, the mythical French escapist, who could not be kept on Devil's Island and whose spirit could not be broken by the oppression of confinement, found methods for maintaining mental and physical alertness, through physical exercise and mental visualization.

These movements can be utilized with or without a knife, at slow, medium or fast speeds, according to the physical/mental ability and coordination of the individual soldier. The knife gives us the availability and training to a method of instilling the physical ability, mental confidence and the fighting spirit to accomplish our mission of survival in hand-to-hand combat, and as a soldier.

These are three phases of knife training utilized in knife fighting. Straight-line attack and counterattacks are utilized during a head-to-head confrontation with the enemy. Master's knife fighting utilizes eight angles of attack and eight circles of counterattack. Counterattack is considered the Master's attack. If two men of equal ability are to meet in battle, the man who initiates an attack, not utilizing the element of surprise, can be evaded and simultaneously counterattacked, as he will expose some area in his defense due to his focus upon an ill-timed attack. One may initiate the physical attack because of an intuitive mental calculation of an attack. Initiating the physical attack becomes a psychological/physical counterattack to a predetermined attack.

The third phase of training is mentally focusing upon a psychological/physical extension of the knife through mental visualization, much as a high-jumper mentally sees himself over the bar, or a football player mentally, emotionally and physically concentrates and feels the winning of a game before going on the field. The knife fighter visualizes the knife as an extension of his body and mind, focusing power in conjunction with breath control, utilizing the knife as an extension of his very being and inner spirit.

There are two primary intervals in knife fighting—outside and inside attacks—calling for different techniques of movement and methods of holding the knife. Outside knife fighting calls for slashing figure eights and darting thrusts to vital areas, similar to a fencer. Inside knife fighting calls for a reverse hold on the knife with the blade running flush with the forearm, concealing the weapon from the eyes of the enemy.

During interval change in attack, the knife fighter flips the knife, changing the hand-hold according to the interval of attack and the situation at hand. Inside knife fighting is considered the most lethal due to the power of the reverse hand-hold position, where the fencer's position exposes the knife to the enemy and makes it easy to dislodge with a kick. The forward fencers' position gives availability to slashing and thrusting while the reverse hand-hold remains concealed and is utilized for stabbing, slashing and ripping. An excellent example of the difference in the power of knife positions is demonstrated by the use of a special training exercise.

Field dress a beef carcass in a standard military field jacket and evaluate the ability to penetrate the field jacket and make an insertion deep enough to be lethal in combat. Utilizing a darting fencers' movement in contrast to an explosive reverse hand-held attack, the reverse position will demonstrate the consistent power and stability needed for penetration and lethal effect during a simulated exercise conducted against the training dummy.

Affording the maximum effective power for lethal insertion, the reverse hand-hold takes priority during the deadly interval of inside knife fighting. Keep in mind knife insertion movements are different movements from knife slashing. Insertion movements are directed at vital targets, a vein or artery penetration, so as to induce unconsciousness and a fast and silent death. The knife has long been a favorite tool for silent interdiction.

The knife fighter attacks with low-leg kicking and sweeping, hand trapping with the lead, empty hand or slashing, blocking and simultaneously attacking the enemy with a lead-hand hold of the knife. Targets are to be hit at as they become exposed to attack, relying upon the reactions and conditioned reflexes of the knife fighter. Targets of priority are the eyes, throat, abdominal area and extended limbs. The knife fighter is trained to spin and redirect the enemy's force and power as he attacks from the enemy's front, evading to the side and spinning to his opponent's rear, using take-downs as he reaches body-to-body contact and following up to the vital areas of insertion. (Refer to vital knife insertion chart.)

I am a strong believer in the use of two knives during knife training and actual close-quarter attack. I have been questioned on the fact of practicality and overkill, but in hand-to-hand combat we have no choice except to kill or be killed, therefore, we must capitalize on every advantage possible. Musashi, the greatest swordsman in the history of Japan, was famous for his two-sworded attack. His school and training methods were called the "strategy of two swords."

The use of two knives gives us the ability to slash, trap and penetrate the enemy's defenses with the lead hand, leaving the back knife in reserve for the final killing blow. Usually the lead knife is in the fencers' position and the back knife is in the reverse hand-hold position prepared for the powerful, inside interval attack. The lead or rear knife can be thrown as a distraction during attack, allowing the knife fighter a diversion so that he may gain that precious moment for him to explode into the enemy from the outside interval to the inside interval, integral to the theory of a six-second, singular attack, totally immobilizing and incapacitating the enemy in one fast and powerful movement.

As a standard rule, the knife is never thrown in combat unless utilized in conjunction with the element of surprise as a distracting or diversionary tactic and only as a last resort. Always keep in mind, once you have thrown the weapon, you have decreased your lethality greatly unless you are an unarmed, hand-to-hand combat expert, of which there are few. Even then the knife becomes a formidable foe to the unarmed expert, for one mistake in movement or timing and the expert could be maimed or killed.

Six Basic Rules to Observe
During Training and Actual Combat

(a) Body position and physical movement during attack

    1. Conceal the weapon from the view of the enemy's eyes.

    2. Observe things that are distant as if they are close at hand, and view things which are close as if they were distant. Maintain 180-degree peripheral vision and 360 degrees of mental awareness and body feelings, intuitively interpreting the movements of the enemy and being constantly aware of a secondary or multiple attack.

    3. Focus on deep breathing and maintain muscle tension in the lower abdominal area; remaining calm in body and mind, but not relaxed.

    4. Slash, don't stab, but when you utilize a stabbing technique, attack a vital area of insertion. (Refer to vital knife insertion chart.)

(b) Mental focus in conjunction with physical movement of the knife

    1. Observe the enemy through half-closed eyes, a partial squint, similar to focusing your eyes upon the small details of an object to receive a clear contrast and sharp visual focus. The knife fighter focuses upon the total sphere of the enemy, never focusing upon one single point of contact

within the enemy's defenses, but observing the point of contact with the blade of the knife mentally, without telegraphing his intentions through body movements, facial expressions, focus of the eyes or intense energy projection, so as not to warn the senses of the enemy to an impending attack; but reacting intuitively to the enemy's movements.

2. Breath control and mental focus of power are essential in creating enough power for a lethal slashing or stabbing movement. Using the psychological impact of a powerful kiai or a terrifying screaming, assault in the face of the enemy can induce a moment of shock or fear causing the enemy to hesitate for a split second, giving the knife fighter the moment of advantage integral to the success of his attack. Or silently, while stalking a sentry, when cover of movement and sound become the integral factors of survival, the knife fighter utilizes a forceful exhale without making a sound except for the force of his exhaled air.

If I were given a mission to train 12 men for an anti-terrorist raid in close-quarter combat techniques, it would be integral that these men could move quietly and quickly and have the ability to eliminate key personnel silently, with a minimum of psychological shock and fear being induced upon the surrounding populace or captives being held hostage. In search of a method of increasing the chances of maintaining control during stabilization and dispersion, in conjunction with decreasing the initial emotional reaction of panic to the sound of gunfire, my choice would have to be a silenced automatic weapon, but in a close, confined area, the automatic weapon can be lethal to the surrounding populace and to the hostages being held captive.

If there is a good probability of reaching body-to-body interval during a silent attack, then the knife can become one of the most deadly and effective tools for interdiction, inducing a minimum of danger to the populace and hostages in the immediate area and providing a silent method of interdiction, stabilization and incapacitation of the enemy.

The integral difference between a lethal and nonlethal attack in hand-to-hand combat is the use of a weapon in a well-trained professional's hand; therefore, the knife becomes an integral weapon to the combat soldier to insure his survival and the accomplishment of his mission.

KNIFE TRAINING

In training for use of the knife, the individual soldier becomes aware of the need for practice without an opponent, normally considered as form or free-form, form being preset and preplanned movements, set to a distinct pattern and rhythm of movement considered to be a simulated attack by the enemy. The knife fighter must vividly visualize, with total emotional content, the attack of the enemy, thereby creating the frame of mind that is needed during actual combat.

The knife fighter begins to train slowly, moving at a minimum of four distinct speeds—quarter, half, three-quarter and full speeds. He begins very slowly, adjusting his mind and body to the new movements being embedded into his subconscious mind, so as to create a conditioned reflex or automatic physical reaction.

As the knife fighter progresses, he begins to increase speed as his body and mind begin to become fluid and the knife no longer moves as a separate entity but becomes an extension of the body, mind and spirit of the knife fighter himself. Once the knife fighter has attained natural movement, he may increase speed and emotional intensity in each movement until finally reaching an emotional, physical peak with each movement, seeming as if he, himself, were in an actual life and death struggle, his very survival depending upon the precision and power of every movement he made.

Wasting not a single motion or bit of vital energy, the knife fighter attacks with economy of motion, conserving his energy until the very last moment, making his insertion lethal as he attacks vital targets of opportunity, exploding into the enemy with low kicking, hand-trapping and slashing, using short, powerful exhalations as he delivers, slashes and stabs.

Form of movement must be broken down into the individual attack, until it becomes a conditioned reflex. It is far better to master one technique than to know ten and master none.

Step-by-step the knife fighter develops his reactions, until finally he progresses from straight-line movements to a master's attack of eight circles at eight different angles. Learning to maintain body balance, rhythm of movement and focus of power, we find that form becomes essentially vital during any development program utilized by the individual soldier. A degree of proficiency must be attained, a perfected, conditioned reflex, so to speak, though no one can achieve total proficiency because of the constant change in relationship to man and his environment. When this degree of proficiency has been developed, then we can progress to free-form, a method of training where the knife fighter envisions simulated attacks while reacting with simulated counterattacks, using an infinite amount of combinations. The knife fighter reacts according to what "feels" natural to him, exploring his imagination and improving upon the basics that he had embedded after endless hours of training.

Use of a wooden or rubber knife is suggested during the initial, basic knife training. Progression to the live blade is essential for that actual "feel" of the individual's combat tool. Just as a soldier should eat, sleep and defecate with his rifle in hand, so should the individual soldier consider his knife not only as an essential tool for his survival but as a weapon to insure his effectiveness in combat. The integral difference between a lethal and nonlethal technique is a weapon.

The knife has long been considered a maiming or killing weapon and, therefore, the individual soldier must take great precautions while training so as to insure his own safety during form training and simulated attacks from a training partner. If actual mastery of the knife is expected, then one must expect to train with a live blade, for there is no substitute for actual combat.

In this book we are contrasting form with actual application of movement itself, the third phase of training being actual freesparring with the wooden blade and progressing to a form of freefighting using a live blade.

These methods of training have been utilized by Asian warriors for over 2,000 years. The study of form can be a great asset during confinement or periods of isolation, allowing the individual soldier to maintain physical fitness and mental alertness and focusing upon combat readiness.

Some instructors feel that there is no place for form during training but all methods of fighting were discovered and developed from some mental form, therefore there is no technique without form. Techniques are created from the imagination and are initially expressed physically, through some type of physical movement. The ability to create and progress individually and internally is an essential factor for maintaining motivation during periods of isolation or confinement. The self-confidence developed by the individual soldier through this type of training can lead him to the virtue of patience during isolation, especially to guerilla warfare where it is essential to outlast the opponent while remaining in isolation for extended periods of time. Instead of this bringing about a negative reaction, the soldier utilizes his time for personal development and focus of awareness.

Just as it is essential that the combat soldier keep his weapon combat-ready, so is it essential that he maintain a physical/mental combat readiness.

Those men who say there is no need for hand-to-hand combat are not aware of the discretion in use of weapons during different intervals of attack. At 25 yards in thick foliage, grenades and automatic weapons are the weapons of choice but in a foxhole crowded with soldiers or in a room or confined area filled with hostages and civilians, the knife must supercede the grenade.

Musashi, the greatest swordsman in the history of Japan, stated in his guide to strategy, *A BOOK OF FIVE RINGS*, that "From inside fortifications, the gun has no equal among weapons. It is the supreme weapon on the field before the ranks clash, but once swords are crossed the gun becomes useless."

The handgun must still be considered the most appropriate weapon for close-quarter attacks even as ranks clash, but as a backup weapon or a tool of silent interdiction and, in certain isolated incidents, utilized in preference to an automatic weapon or a large, cumbersome rifle, the knife becomes one of the most effective and lethal methods of close-quarter attack, second only to a handgun. Very important is awareness of time factors in relationship to the physical reaction time and mental alertness both on the part of the knife fighter and the enemy. The knife trainee must take all factors into consideration, contrasting them with the type, angle and stability of terrain, atmospheric condition and close-quarter visibility.

His ability to move quickly and explode effectively are based greatly upon ground conditions. Knife training should be conducted under all atmospheric conditions, in all types of terrain and at critical times of the day, such as just before sunrise when the enemy soldier is normally just awakening and not mentally alert or physically prepared to react to the attack of the infiltrator; when the attacker's night vision is well adjusted to the terrain and light factors. Immediately after ingestion of food, the enemy's energy is utilized for digestion which slows down his physical reactions, providing a critical moment for attack. Similar tactics are using terrain and the psychological effect of an attack, such as high ground to the enemy's low ground position. The sun to your back at sunrise or sunset during close-quarter combat and shadows of the night for concealment of movement, increase the chance to utilize the element of surprise. Any period of light change from darkness to light or light to darkness must be considered as advantages to be utilized against the enemy instead of disadvantages that may cause the guerilla fighter himself disorientation: such as in the middle of the night when a flare is tripped and explodes, lighting up the immediate combat area. Assuming that you are in a predetermined field of fire, you have but seconds to react. If both eyes remain open during the exposure to the flare's light, the guerilla fighter's night vision is immediately destroyed and it will take approximately 30 minutes for the visual purple to chemically take effect within the eyes, restoring his full night vision. Therefore, the trained soldier must learn to react and take advantage of situations in hopes that the enemy himself is caught wide-eyed and by surprise. Keeping your rifle aiming eye closed and the opposite eye open during light exposure, one has availability to visual observation during the flare's light exposure, giving him an advantage in reacting to situations at hand. As the light dissipates and darkness once again engulfs the battlefield, the trained soldier utilizes his closed eye, now at least 50 percent effective and still able to react to darkness or light, thus capitalizing on elements and factors available to his adaptability. This is common knowledge to all combat soldiers, but capitalized on during the action at the objective by very few. This type of training and utilization of the elements and psychological frames of mind, disadvantageous to the enemy, are essential factors in sentry stalking while using the knife as a weapon of silent interdiction.

It is quite possible to be operating in areas which are partially lighted for security reasons but you will be concealed within darkness and shadows, only to appear for the brief and critical moment, then disappear again, engulfed by darkness. This method of operating in light then quickly to darkness while still maintaining visual focus in both situations without readjusting to the light exposure, calls for utilization of this basic technique.

Common sense, a creative ingenuity, sound basic soldiering and the ability to adapt to all situations at anytime and anyplace in the world, are the essential elements needed for success as an unconventional warfare operative.

PSYCHOLOGICAL-PHYSICAL FAMILIARIZATION
OF A WEAPON THROUGH VISUALIZATION —

Chemuen Sul

Relaxed meditation and visualization have been studied and used for thousands of years all over the world, the ability to ease hypertension and focus mental concentration for increased visualization. Visualization is termed as a mental picture screen with the subconscious mind as its computer index of mental images and knowledge, with the conscious mind being the visual image screen and the center of awareness. By embedding visual images through vivid visualization of the objective at hand, we can induce a subconscious reaction, thereby enhancing the ability to react with a conditioned reflex.

Just as a football player visualizes his plays and associates numbers or a high diver visualizes his movements just prior to diving, the knife fighter visualizes first the weapon as the extension of his mind and body. Second, he visualizes his training technique for memory and familiarization of combat fighting techniques; and third, he envisions actual combat with single and multiple attacks, mentally and emotionally, actually seeing and feeling the battle and gaining a sense of well-being from mentally winning. Vince Lombardi of the Green Bay Packers once said winning wasn't everything—it was the only thing; and it most certainly applies to this situation where the individual soldier in hand-to-hand combat has but two choices, to win or die.

It is essential to gain a sense of feeling for your combat weapon. A weapon which is too heavy or cumbersome restricting your mobility or feels awkward to grip, can throw the well-trained fighting machine into an uncomfortable and awkward position. A mental and physical familiarization of the weapon can decrease this sense of uneasiness. This method may be used in the familiarization of any weapon for combat use.

Start in a relaxed position, sitting cross-legged on the ground, kneeling while resting the buttocks on the heels of the feet, sitting in a chair or standing. The prone position will induce sleep in the beginners, so its use is discouraged until better mental control is gained.

Begin by relaxing the body and clearing the mind of outside thoughts:

1. Focus your eyes at a fixed object, preferably at a 45-degree angle to the front and at an angle causing the eyes to look up and inducing a heaviness of the eyelids.

2. Take 25 deep breaths, forcing the air deep into the lower abdomen and holding it in, exhaling slowly and relaxed, to a mental count of three.

3. Mentally begin to relax the physical body, starting at your toes and working your way up each individual muscle and joint, mentally suggesting relaxation and a body sensation of heaviness.

4. The individual then reinstates relaxation three times with a mental command, visualizing his eyelids closing as if they were two shades on a window.

5. The knife fighter then visualizes himself standing at the top of a flight of stairs, thinking only of the number nine. With each step down, the individual reinstates mentally his relaxation and control of concentration. Counting down from nine to one with each step he mentally visualizes and verbally reinstates relaxation and focus of mind.

6. At the completion of this mental exercise, the knife fighter should be in a relaxed and focused state of mind. He may have to repeat this mental process three to six times to reach deep relaxation. Once relaxed, the knife fighter mentally envisions the knife as an extension of his body and mind, suggesting an inseparable oneness and feel for the weapon. The weapon may be held or visualized without physical contact. This method of training can be used during a recall process of fighting techniques or as a method of relaxing and discovering new techniques from vivid visualization of simulated attackers.

7. After two to 10 minutes of concentration, mentally relax, clear your mind and mentally suggest a sense of physical/mental well-being. Suggest you will comprehend, retain and recall all of your objectives during this process of visualization three times mentally, then open your eyes, feeling refreshed and alert.

A MASTER'S THEORY OF STRATEGY AND MOVEMENT

"Eight Points of the Circle"

NOTE: The eighth trigram of the *I Ching* signifies the completion of all things—the universe as a whole. In man, it signifies the merging of the body and mind, attaining a spirit one with the universe; mastering the self so that one can control his movement through life.

"Man is but a moment in the Universe"

In hwarangdo, there are 108 different weapons systems. All unarmed and armed techniques, their theory of movement and strategy of application, are based upon the same geometrical configuration.

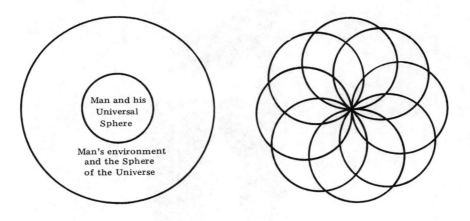

This geometrical configuration symbolizes man and his relationship to constant change in the Universe.

These geometrical configurations represent man and his relationship to the everchanging environment of the universe. Equally they represent the angles of defense and attack, and represent the theory of physical movement and mental perception of the master strategist and his application of technique in hwarangdo. The continual motion represented by the eight circles is termed the "continuous circle of 1,000 attacks." This strategy of continuous "hit and run" is utilized as the basis of all tactical movement and application of technique in the 108 weapons systems of hwarangdo.

Each man is surrounded by an imaginary sphere, considered his personal territorial space. This space is measured by the length of the individual's arms, in a circumference of 360 degrees forming his circle of defense, a personal perimeter. When confronted with the enemy in close-quarters hand-to-hand combat, the space and distance between opponents, considered the interval gap, becomes the number one factor in our ability to interpret and react to the enemy's movement.

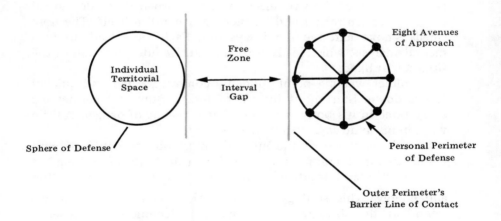

The combat soldier must maintain constant control of the tempo or rhythm of the enemy's movements and the distance or interval during defense and attack, so that he may control the situation and create the opportunity to bridge the interval gap and enter the enemy's sphere of defense at will.

Two factors are of primary concern—time and distance. If these factors are controlled, then the direction of motion can be controlled. Einstein's theory of time, distance and relativity is an example of this type of strategy. In essence, there is no time or distance, only constant motion; a straight line with a curve to it, infinitely a circle, the "continuous circle of 1,000 attacks." A warrior who masters this theory in body and mind is said to be a phantom of the battlefield who can battle 1,000 men and win.

No man is allowed to enter another man's personal, territorial space unexpectedly or with ill intent. In actual hand-to-hand combat, the enemy has but one intent—his opponent's death. Therefore, the best reaction is a premeditated attack or instantaneous counterattack before the enemy is able to launch his actual offensive. This first strike capability and its probability of success is based primarily on the element of surprise. To increase this perceptive ability, the individual must rely heavily on the sixth sense, or his intuition, often referred to by soldiers as a "deep gut feeling." Each of the five senses must be sharpened and developed through concentration and considered a mind in itself. The nose smells smoke and the mind says fire. Each sense leads us to a mental analysis, which leads us to an intuitive interpretation of the situation at hand.

A soldier walking point suddenly comes to a halt and quickly squats down. Starting at the tip of his sternum and permeating every bone in his body, he senses a deep feeling of danger. A little voice in his mind says, "Halt—danger!"

This inner voice of the intuition must not be confused with mental rationalizing; for the trained warrior thinks of nothing but his objective, and negative rationalizing only deters concentration and energy. This strategy is termed the technique of a "single mind" or the strategy of "no mind, no technique"—in essence only reaction, a conditioned reflex. This man functions not through negative reasoning, but through willpower, and focus of concentration in a positive mental focus.

When the combat soldier is confronted by multiple-man attack, he must maintain a 360-degree, defensive perimeter of mental awareness. Mentally, the knife fighter must visualize the basic eight avenues of approach. He must remain physically mobile and ready to react to multiple attacks in accordance to the rhythm, timing and speed of the enemy, with a primary focus of

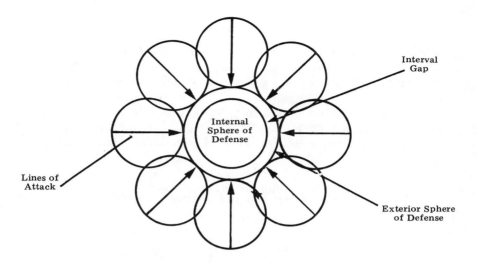

Each of the eight spheres represents the defensive perimeters of the possible eight avenues of approach and the enemy's contact zones.

controlling the tempo of the battle in a cycle of consecutive and successful attacks, gaining positive momentum with each decisive win.

If one or more assailants attack at once, then the knife fighter must choose the weakest and most readily available target, attack and redirect the enemy's body into the oncoming path of the other assailants, causing momentary delay and serving as a body shield to the knife fighter. This brief confusion gives the knife fighter that essential moment to gain control of the tempo and rhythm of the fight and therefore allows time for him to perceive the center of the multiple-enemy attack and evade its onslaught as he circles to the outside and center of the attacking mass.

Another strategy is based upon the theory of the "circle and point." In this method of attack, the enemy is visualized geometrically as square and the movement of evasion is based upon a circular counterattack. A direct frontal or straight-line attack represents the "point." The counterattack represents the circle, giving availability to an instantaneous counterattack and total evasion. Hard, straight-line attacks are countered by fast, circular counterattacks and fast, circular attacks are best countered by hard, straight-line counterattacks.

A master's attack is often considered the most simple and direct attack possible. Utilizing full economy of motion, the knife fighter conserves his energy for the final movement of the actual hit, focusing every essence of his being into and through the point of contact.

A simple sidestep and direct straight-line attack can be the counterattack which is the fastest, most economical and most effective of all reactions. The diagram below is an example of such a counterattack.

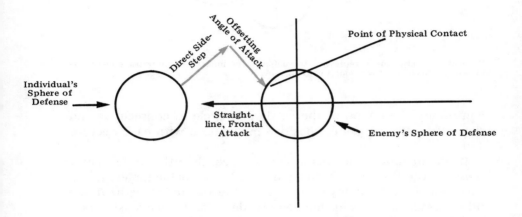

"DIRECT, STRAIGHT-LINE COUNTERATTACK AT AN OFFSETTING ANGLE"

The knife fighter initiates or evades attack by sidestepping to the direct left or right of the enemy's attack; blocking, trapping and redirecting the enemy's straight-line frontal assault. He then counters with a straight-line, offsetting angle attack, avoiding the enemy's attack and penetrating an exposure in the defense of the enemy as his mind and body are focused on and through the point of contact.

Circular attacks give availability to continual motion, and develop power through centrifugal force. Whipping in at leg or low level, attacking the midsection or middle level, or whipping in at the head at high level—these spinning techniques cause confusion in the enemy's mind and generate a tremendous follow-through of power.

42

The diagram below demonstrates a circular attack at an offsetting angle.

"CIRCULAR ATTACK AT AN OFFSETTING ANGLE"

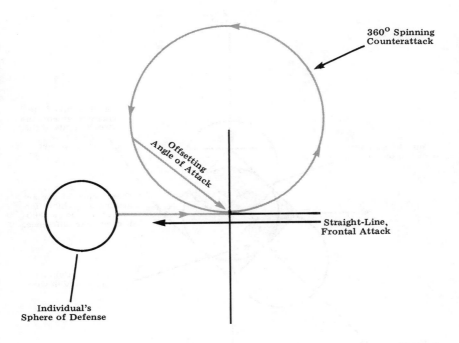

360° Spinning
Counterattack

Offsetting
Angle of Attack

Straight-Line,
Frontal Attack

Individual's
Sphere of Defense

Slashing, sweeping, in conjunction with powerful, low kicking, the knife fighter shoots to the immediate side of the enemy's attack, spinning 360 degrees, building power through centrifugal force, shooting to the immediate rear or opposite side of the enemy, thus trapping the head and redirecting it in a circular motion while slashing the neck and sweeping or reaping the legs in a powerful, spinning throw. Following with the continual motion of the circular movement, the knife fighter hits hard, evades and prepares for a new offensive or counteroffensive, based upon the movement of the enemy.

Inside-fighting is considered a lethal contact zone, and outside-fighting is considered the nonlethal contact zone. The success of the inside attack is based upon the ability of the attacker to utilize the element of surprise and strike at will, capitalizing on targets of opportunity and focusing total power into vital striking. Contact zones are controlled by interval spacing, and just as a soldier has predetermined fields of fire, so must the strategist have predetermined zones of contact.

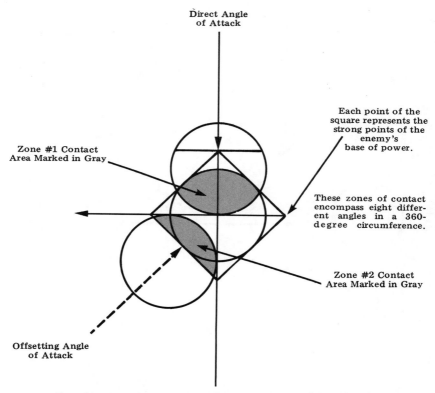

"PREDETERMINED ZONES OF CONTACT"

Direct Angle
of Attack

Each point of the
square represents the
strong points of the
enemy's
base of power.

Zone #1 Contact
Area Marked in Gray

These zones of contact
encompass eight differ-
ent angles in a 360-
degree circumference.

Zone #2 Contact
Area Marked in Gray

Offsetting Angle
of Attack

Zone #1 represents the areas of contact at a direct angle of approach.
Zone #2 represents the area of contact at an indirect angle of approach.

Control of man's center of balance or base of power is focused through mental concentration and breath control. This center of energy power is one to three inches below the navel, and in the deep squat position the body can be divided by imaginary lines, their axis being the center of man's base of power and body balance.

This imaginary axis is considered the center of all power in the studies of breath control and focus of power; the center of man's energy field, or ki, in the study of hwarangdo.

Ki is contained in all animate and inanimate objects. It is created by the contraction-expansion rate or dipole movement of the atom, a nonelectrical energy sometimes termed as bio-plasmic energy, the very life force of existence itself.

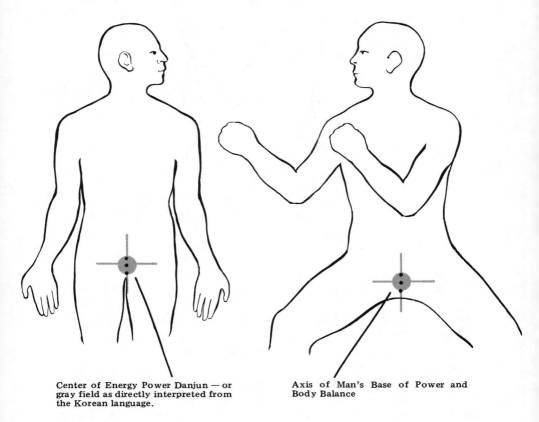

Center of Energy Power Danjun — or gray field as directly interpreted from the Korean language.

Axis of Man's Base of Power and Body Balance

These imaginary lines and their axis of power can be moved to other portions of the body or extended outside of the body and projected through space by thought, such as a fencer thrusting through his target or a fighter punching through his opponent. The generation and control of this power is focused through breathing and mental visualization, extended from the very ground itself,

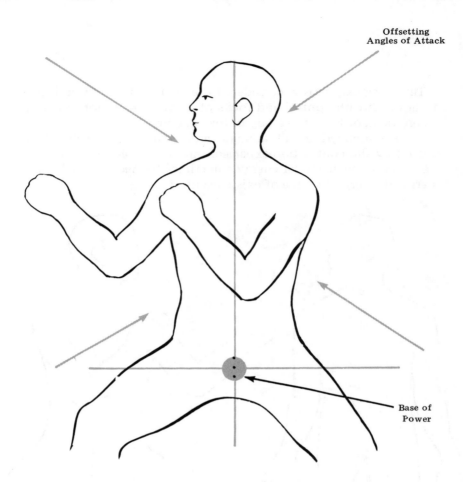

Offsetting
Angles of Attack

Base of
Power

through his body and through the point of contact as he forcefully exhales and creates the power extension of body and mind.

Offsetting angles of attack are usually the avenues of approach, exposing vital targets of opportunity in the weakness of the enemy's perimeter of defense. They are also the weakest angles of balance and power in the enemy's base of balance. Have an assistant assume a fighting stance and you assume a fighting stance at any of the four offsetting 45-degree angles of attack in relationship to the positive lines of power and the positive axis of the base. You will clearly see the openings in your opponent's defense. These are the primary angles of offsetting attack and the weakest lines of power in your opponent's base and perimeter of defense.

The following diagram shows the angles of attack and their areas of physical contact.

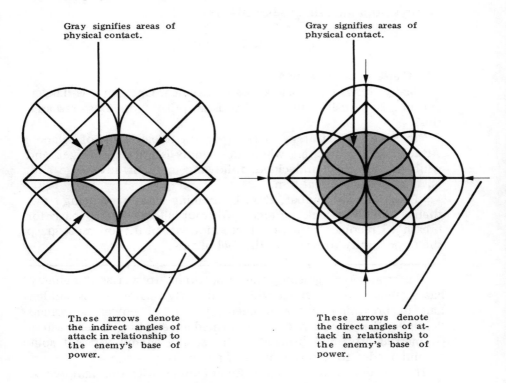

Gray signifies areas of physical contact.

Gray signifies areas of physical contact.

These arrows denote the indirect angles of attack in relationship to the enemy's base of power.

These arrows denote the direct angles of attack in relationship to the enemy's base of power.

Note: Compare the areas of physical contact utilizing an indirect angle of attack and the areas of contact when utilizing a direct angular attack. The chance of counterattack by the enemy is greatly increased during direct angular attack.

In actual hand-to-hand combat, the individual soldier must maintain mental awareness in a 360-degree defensive perimeter and physical mobility so that he reacts with the proper movement and counterattack. Mentally, the knife fighter must visualize the basic eight avenues of approach and be ready to react physically to multiple attacks in accordance to the rhythm, timing and speed of the enemy; with a primary focus of controlling the tempo of the battle in a cycle of consecutive and successful attacks, gaining positive momentum with each decisive win—Win or die!

A BOOK OF FIVE RINGS
A Guide To Strategy

by Miyamoto Musashi (1584—1645)*

"The Fire Book"

"To Cause Loss of Balance"
"Many things can cause a loss of balance. One cause is danger, another is hardship and another is surprise. You must research this.
"In large-scale strategy, it is important to cause loss of balance. Attack without warning where the enemy is not expecting it, and while his spirit is undecided, following up your advantage and, having the lead, defeat him.
"Or, in single combat, start by making a show of being slow, then suddenly attack strongly. Without allowing him space for breath to recover from the fluctuation of spirit, you must grasp the opportunity to win. Get the feel of this."

The strategy of grasping the opportunity to win as the enemy has a fluctuation of spirit which is directly related to his sudden halt in breathing and a momentary loss of power is termed "clasping the will," a technique termed as secret by Asian masters of martial arts, and utilized to freeze the enemy for that split second needed for a powerful blow and a decisive win.

The left eye is said to make direct contact with the right eye of the enemy's power. This gives an interlocking energy chain as the right side of the body is positive and projects energy, while the left side absorbs power and receives energy. As the enemy loses momentary control of his power through loss of breath control, the master robs the enemy of his neutral power by locking on to the energy projection of the enemy's eyes. He sends an energy shock from his lower abdomen by tensing the muscles of the lower

*Miyamoto Musashi was the greatest swordsman in the history of Japan. By the age of 30, he had fought and killed over 60 men in close-quarters combat. Many of these he killed not with the blade of his sword but the edge of his wooden training sword. So fierce was his spirit that he was termed invincible. At the age of 59, after countless samurai battles, with never a loss, Musashi retired to a cave in the mountains near Kyushu. Here, in seclusion, he wrote *Go Rin No Sho (A Book of Five Rings)*. The book is not a thesis on strategy; it is, in Musashi's words, "a guide for men who want to learn strategy." And as a guide always leads, so the contents are always beyond the student's immediate understanding.

abdomen area, forcefully exhaling and mentally visualizing the projection of energy. He locks onto the enemy's will with a clasping sensation in the lower abdomen, very similar to the feeling of two fingers pinching and controlling an object, freezing the enemy for that split second needed for victory. This method of "stealing the enemy's power" was a strategy studied by spies and swordmasters of ancient times. Only in Asia were these metaphysical theories guarded as secrets of state, harbored behind the walls of religious monasteries. Here they are covered in theory alone, analyzed and only partially exposed.

(Quoting from Musashi's *A Book of Five Rings*)

"The Fire Book"

"In this, the Fire Book of the Ni To Ichi school of strategy, I describe fighting as fire.

"In the first place, people think narrowly about the benefit of strategy. By using only their fingertips, they let a contest be decided, as with the folding fan, merely by the span of their forearms. They specialize in the small matter of dexterity, learning such trifles as hand and leg movements with the bamboo practice sword.

"In my strategy, the training for killing enemies is by way of many contests, fighting for survival, discovering the meaning of life and death, learning the way of the sword, judging the strength of attacks and understanding the way of the 'edge and ridge' of the sword.

"You cannot profit from small techniques, particularly when full armor is worn. My way of strategy is the sure method to win when fighting for your life, one man against five or ten. There is nothing wrong with the principle, 'One man can beat ten, so a thousand can beat ten thousand.' You must research this. Of course, you cannot assemble a thousand or ten thousand men for everyday training. But you can become a master of strategy by training alone with a sword, so that you can understand the enemy's stratagems, his strength and resources, and come to appreciate how to apply strategy to beat ten thousand enemies.

"Any man who wants to master the essence of my strategy

must research diligently, training morning and evening. Thus can he polish his skill, become free from self, and realize extraordinary ability. He will come to possess miraculous power.

"This is the practical result of strategy."

There are two types of student in the study of martial arts. One is the student who begins training empty of physical techniques and knowledge of strategy and develops until he reaches a point of proficiency where he becomes filled and cluttered with techniques and thought, striving to plan strategy and physical reactions to the enemy's movements. The other is the master student, who is void of thought and physical technique, but is a mere reaction and conditioned reflex to the enemy's movements. To claim the title "Master" and not to attach students is to become fixed and stagnant and this is not in compatibility with the constant change of man and his physical/mental relationship to the constant change of his environment. Therefore, there are no true masters, only students and master students, for there can be no limits to the accomplishments possible within the lives and minds of men.

THREE PHASES OF STRATEGY

There are three primary phases of reaction to attack related to the three different types of strategy.

Phase #1—Escape and Evasion:

When the interval gap is bridged by the enemy during attack, the individual's territorial space comes in contact with the enemy's territorial space, and each individual must come to defense of his personal perimeter. One phase of strategy is evasion.

In Asia, this method of training consisted of evading the attacker and controlling the tempo of the situation, based upon the religious and moral beliefs stressed by the Buddhist doctrine. It teaches never to take a life, for all living creatures were believed to be reincarnations of former ancestors. This method of training was studied primarily by the Buddhist monks. Bear in mind, though, one of Mao Tse Tung's strategies in guerrilla warfare was to "attack while retreating."

Apache Indians of North America were master tacticians when it came to this method of strategy. The cavalry would chase the

Indians on horseback at a full pace into the mountains and the Indians and cavalry would run their horses to death. The Indians would then clean the horses' intestines of matter and fill them with fresh blood. With a substantial reserve of liquids needed for survival, the Apache warriors would continue on. Knowing the terrain from birth, the Indians would soon make it to water, then vanish into the mountains. Short on water, with no method of quick return, the soldiers would soon die of thirst and exposure, without a single man coming into close-quarters combat.

An example of this type of strategy on a large scale was the Russian retreat during the German offensive of World War II. Again, nature and the elements were utilized as a tactical advantage, and the Russian withdrawal was the Germans' eventual defeat.

To exhaust the enemy's offensive through constant evasion and movement is a basic concept of unconventional warfare, and can lead the many-times-outnumbered guerrilla fighter to victory through evasion alone.

The greatest victory comes without conflict or confusion.

Phase #2—Stabilization and Control:

If the individual's territorial space is entered unexpectedly, he must react in accordance with the type and intent of attack. Phase #2 of strategy is stabilization and control. This method of strategy is demonstrated by the use of unarmed methods of self-defense orientated towards control, such a jujitsu, aikido, hapkido and judo. The use of the bo staff, middle and short stick, the cane and fan are examples of this type of training, and were usually reserved for the noble class of Asia. Their purpose is self-preservation and physical/mental development. These were very refined studies, orientated towards control, and were considered art forms. These men were trained never to take a life without cause, and stood by this code with great honor.

Code of Reaction:
(a) No man was allowed to touch or grab a warrior or nobleman trained in the arts. Techniques of control were utilized, such as joint-locking, throwing, and pressure points to deter aggression.
(b) If the enemy attempted to strike a warrior, then blood could be drawn to deter further attack. Striking techniques, such as kicking and punching, were utilized.

(c) If a warrior was struck and blood drawn, then he was instructed to use joint-breaking techniques to disable the attacker and deter further aggression.

(d) If the enemy attempted to break or crush the warrior bones, then they were instructed to kill the enemy.

This code was followed for thousands of years in Asia, and is still carried on by some warrior sects of today.

Phase #3—Neutralization:

This phase of strategy encompasses attack and counterattack, with a primary objective of destroying the enemy in combat. This type of training was used by the military for the development of its generals and leaders in the warring arts. Here, all forms of physical and mental training and discipline were studied. Secret methods of strategy were studied for the purpose of developing armies and conducting war.

This phase of strategy encompasses such physical techniques as too yuk gi, tearing of human flesh with bare hands, and the 38 categories of killing techniques in hwarangdo, termed hwarang samship yuksul bob.

The study of 108 weapons systems is termed waygong in hwarangdo. The use of weapons in combat, such as short and long sword, stick fighting with all lengths, bow and arrow, crossbow, knife fighting, dirk, dagger or dart throwing, spear and chain fighting, are examples of this type of training and strategy.

Such advanced studies as garrotes, poisons, blow-guns, stealth and concealment, stalking and silent killings were studied as tactics by the superhuman Sulsa, medieval agents of espionage utilizing the techniques and ancient art of un ship bob, the Korean counterpart of Japanese ninjitsu, the "art of invisibility."

These methods of training and theories of strategy were developed for the purpose of internal security and aggressively defeating the enemy on the battlefield.

Without strategy, the individual cannot apply technique. It is like having a car, but not knowing how to drive. There are no limitations to strategy, for the number of reactions is infinite. If you know only how to turn a car left, what will you do when you come to a right turn?

CHANGING THE KNIFE

The knife fighter holds the weapon in a lead hand reverse hold, maintaining balance and control from the middle of the blade, tensing the little finger and ring finger of the right hand, while maintaining a loose and fluid control of the weapon with the middle finger, index finger and thumb. Notice the left hand is protecting the face and throat while the lead forearm is protecting the chest and body. This is to afford the knife fighter every aspect of safety during the movement of the knife. The knife fighter then raises the weapon towards him while pointing the index finger of the right hand and flips the knife forward. Relaxing his grip and opening his hand, he turns the knife 180 degrees into a lead hand forward hold, similar to a fencer. He then raises his right arm again while flipping and rotating the weapon with his thumb and index finger back in a reverse hold. This exercise, in conjunction with changing hands with the weapon, is utilized to train the knife fighter in all aspects and positions of knife fighting. This exercise should be performed 1,000 times per day until a fluid, rhythmic movement of the knives can be attained.

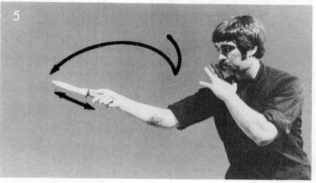

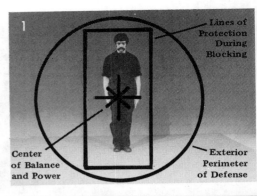

Lines of Protection During Blocking

Center of Balance and Power

Exterior Perimeter of Defense

FOUR BLOCKS AND FORWARD ROLL

The knife fighter stands at the position of attention with the knives concealed. He then draws his left hand and elbow up across the front of the body while simultaneously lifting the right leg and protecting the midsection with the right arm. He then shoots forward, performing a high-rising block with his right hand blocking the attacker's movement with the edge of the blade. The right leg is in a cocking position in front of the body, protecting the groin and ready for leg checking and counterkicking. As the knife comes into its final position for the high-rising block, the right foot steps forward and the knife fighter assumes a back fighting stance with 80 percent of his weight on his rear leg. The knife fighter then draws both hands up in front of the body and crosses them in front of the body to perform a double-inside block. He then circles the knives to the outside and performs a double-outside block. Next he brings the knives into position for a low block. Then raising the left hand and performing a high-rising block, the knife fighter shoots forward, moving the knives back into their original position, concealed and riding along the inner edge of the forearm. He drives forward and executes a forward roll, exploding back into his original knife-fighting position. This time, the weight is distributed more evenly, with 60 percent of the weight on the front leg and the back toe raised slightly, very similar to the fencer's position, so that the knife fighter can explode into his next attack.

57

BACK STANCE
FIGHTING POSITION

Bearing 80 percent of his weight upon the back leg, using the lead leg as a checking/counterkicking weapon, the knife fighter attacks in a figure-eight motion, stepping and darting with explosive quickness into the attacker.

Note the circling and protecting moves used by the body at all times. The opposite hand is used here.

The attacker parries the opponent's thrust with an inside circular movement and follows up with a thrust to his body.

CONTINUED

HAND TRAP, ARM SLASH AND DOWN THRUST

The knife fighter assumes the back fighting stance. He then adjusts his weight to a front fighting stance, while simultaneously performing a low block with the right hand and a high-rising block with the left hand. The knife fighter shoots forward, explod-

ing into the enemy, while simultaneously slashing up with the right hand and trapping the enemy's lead hand down with his left hand. He then comes into final position while performing a down strike into the enemy's sub-clavian area.

HAND
TRAP, ARM SLASH
AND DOWN THRUST

64

HAND TRAP, ARM SLASH AND SIDE THRUST

The knife fighter assumes a ready, mobile position while the knife attacker thrusts forward from the fencing position with a left-handed straight thrust. The knife fighter sidesteps to his direct right while simultaneously blocking, trapping and redirecting the attacking hand of the enemy. He then rotates his body towards the direct front of the enemy

while maintaining control of the wrist and weapon. The knife fighter then slashes across the brachial artery, into the lower biceps, causing the enemy to drop the weapon. Using full economy of motion, he immediately thrusts the weapon directly into the throat of the attacker. This movement should be fluid, well-timed and centered directly into vital areas.

HAND
TRAP, ARM SLASH
AND SIDE THRUST

COUNTERATTACK AGAINST A STRAIGHT KNIFE THRUST

The knife fighter steps left, clearing his body of the weapon, blocking and trapping the attacker's thrust.

He slashes the stomach as he moves. For this, the fighter uses a straight side slash, turning the knife over on the way back, utilizing an inverted stomach slash.

The fighter's hand traps the enemy's knife hand down, bringing the knife hand out in a circular motion, around and down into the neck of the attacker.

COUNTERATTACK AGAINST A STRAIGHT KNIFE THRUST

360-DEGREE
SPINNING NECK-
SLASH AND REVERSE STAB

The knife fighter sidesteps a
downward knife thrust, blocking and
trapping the attacking knife hand.

He slashes the neck as he steps in,
slashing and spinning 360 degrees
continuously in a forward motion toward the attacker.

The fighter slashes his hand in a
downward motion across the opponent's face while trapping any counterattack.

The knife fighter follows up with
a downward stab to the attacker's
neck.

75

360-DEGREE SPINNING NECK-SLASH AND REVERSE STAB

NECK SLASH, GROIN THRUST AND HOP-SKIPPING SIDE KICK

The knife fighter sidesteps a straight thrust to the face, using a circular outside block and trapping with the lead hand.

He steps and pulls the attacker's arm, slashing the neck, rotating the hips to the rear and low-thrusting to the groin.

The fighter rotates and thrusts the hips to the front, thrusting up and ripping out.

As the opponent falls back, the knife fighter executes a hop-skip-leg-breaking technique, kicking to the head, midsection or legs. In actual combat, the individual soldier should focus his kicks from the enemy's belt down to his toes and ankles, thereby giving himself greater stability and power in view of a probable counter-attack or multiple-man attack.

NECK SLASH, GROIN THRUST AND HOP-SKIPPING SIDE KICK

RIGHT STEP MANTIS BLOCK WITH ARM-SLASH/LEG-SWEEP AND A FOLLOW-UP

The knife fighter sidesteps to the right of a left-handed knife thrust, keeping his free hand and elbow close to his body for blocking protection.

He blocks and traps the thrust with a loose-wrist-hand-trap, controlling the attacker's wrist.

Rotating his hips, the fighter slashes the brachial area of the upper arm, causing the attacker to drop his blade.

The knife fighter thrusts to the groin and the neck, sweeping the lead leg, for a strong takedown.

He follows up with a neck thrust and elbow break across the knee, focusing control in the wrist joint with a reverse-come-along wrist lock.

**RIGHT STEP
MANTIS BLOCK
WITH ARM-SLASH/LEG-
SWEEP AND A FOLLOW-UP**

CROSS-LEG
REAPING THROW

The knife fighter sidesteps a right-handed knife thrust, blocking and trapping the attacker's wrists as he moves.

He performs an inverted arm-slash across the brachial region of the lower biceps area, causing the attacker to drop his knife.

The fighter rotates and turns the knife blade. He slashes the neck, thrusts to the kidneys, thrusts to the back of the neck and rotates the attacking knife hand with an outside wrist-breaking technique.

The knife fighter makes a circular motion with the knife blade and thrusts to the attacker's neck while performing a cross-leg reaping throw.

He follows up with a thrust to the neck and an elbow-break across the knee.

CONTINUED

CONTINUED

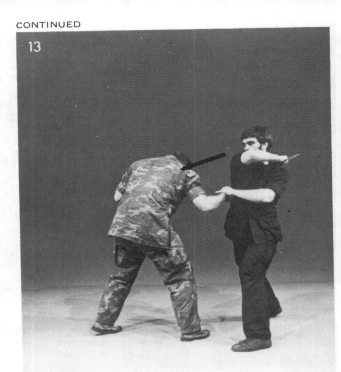

CONTINUED

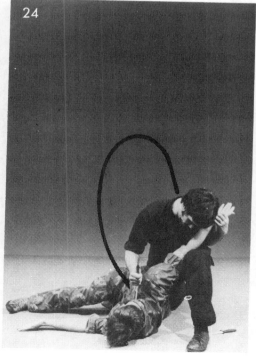

CROSS-LEG
REAPING THROW

CONTINUED

97

BACK-SPINNING
GROIN THRUST

The knife fighter sidesteps the attacker's downward thrust, blocking, trapping and redirecting the attack.

He slashes the stomach and turns the blade in motion, using an inverted throat slash.

The fighter spins to the outside and back, thrusting to the attacker's groin.

CONTINUED

BACK-SPINNING GROIN THRUST

BACK-SPINNING STRAIGHT THRUST

The knife fighter evades a downward thrust by back-stepping, blocking, trapping and redirecting the attacker's thrust.

He then darts to the right rear of the attacker, pulling and jerking the attacking arm to his side and rear.

The fighter then explodes across the attacker's front, using an inverted stomach slash.

While still controlling the attacker's wrist, he thrusts the attacking arm to the rear and spins, slashing the neck and kicking the shin with the lead leg.

The knife fighter changes the knife (in a flipping motion) during his circular attack and thrusts the blade into the attacker's midsection using a reverse spin.

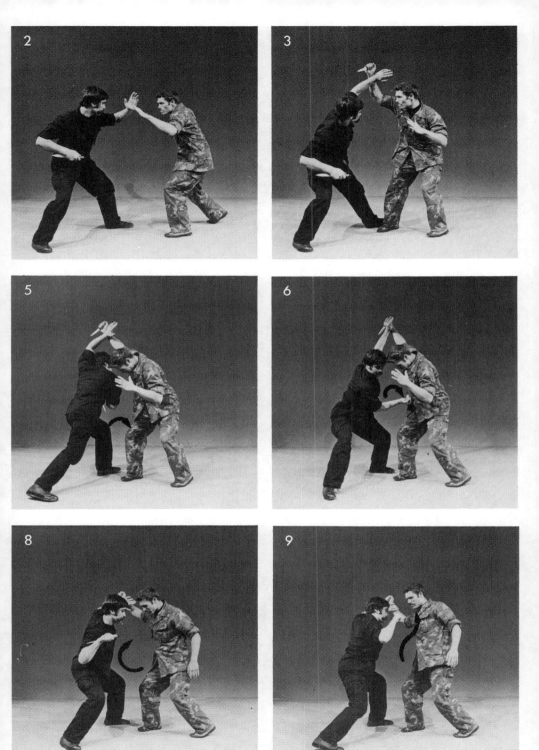

CONTINUED

BACK-SPINNING
STRAIGHT THRUST

SPINNING WING THROW

The knife fighter stands in a ready, mobile position with two knives, both held in the reverse hold position. The knife attacker stands in the fencer's position with a rear hand reverse hold. The knife attacker steps forward with his right foot while executing a down thrust with his right arm. The knife fighter sidesteps to the enemy's direct right rear while simultaneously slashing, blocking and redirecting the attacking arm of the enemy with his lead left hand. He executes a right-hand slash down across the side of the neck of the opponent. Bringing the arm down into the middle of the body, he then thrusts it forward again into the throat of the enemy, using the edge of the blade as the focus of the thrusting motion. He then steps to the immediate rear of the enemy while shooting his left arm up and underneath the enemy's left arm. Once in this rear position, the knife fighter can utilize innumberable types of attacks. Here he continues in a 360-degree spin. While thrusting the blade of the left hand into the enemy's throat, he executes a left-leg reaping throw, while driving the upper portion of the enemy's body towards the ground. He then spins 180 degrees while executing a down thrust into the enemy's groin.

SPINNING WING THROW

113

360-DEGREE BACK-SPINNING COUNTERATTACK

The knife fighter evades a right-hand down thrust of the enemy by sidestepping to the enemy's direct right, simultaneously blocking, trapping and redirecting the attack with the lead left hand. The knife fighter spins 360 degrees and counterattacks to the back of the neck in a powerful whipping slash.

Note: Due to the dangerous body position shown in the final frames and the obvious exposure to counterattack, this movement should be performed extremely fast and at 90-degree angles to the direct, straight-line attack, spinning and countering. Notice the bulge in the right leg of the knife fighter's black uniform. His hat and shas had been stuffed in his pant legs for tight padding and leg protection and, in this instance, protecting himself from counterattack and possible injury. A possible set-up.

RIGHT SPINNING LEG SWEEP

The knife fighter assumes a back fighting stance with a lead hand reverse hold. The knife attacker assumes a front stance with a backhand fencer's hold. The knife attacker then explodes forward with his left leg while thrusting towards the knife fighter's midsection. The knife fighter immediately sidesteps to the enemy's left rear while simultaneously blocking, trapping and redirecting the thrust of the enemy. He then performs an inverted stomach slash. While spinning 180 degrees to the enemy's rear and executing a backspinning throat thrust, the knife fighter then traps the wrist and weapon of the enemy while sweeping his leg out from the rear. As the enemy falls, the knife fighter maintains control of the wrist and weapon.

While dropping all his weight down into a kneeling position with his left foot extended and his left knee raised, the knife fighter breaks the arm of the attacker and thrusts the knife to the enemy's throat.

CONTINUED

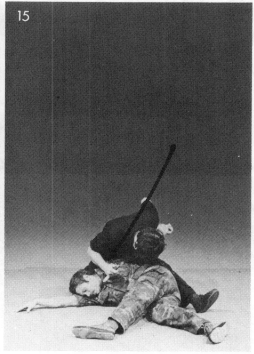

RIGHT SPINNING LEG SWEEP

121

LEFT SPINNING LEG SWEEP

The knife fighter assumes a ready, mobile position with the knife in the rear hand and reverse-hold position. The knife attacker stands in the fencing position with a back hand fencer's hold. The knife attacker shoots forward while thrusting to the midsection of the knife fighter. The knife fighter sidesteps to the right rear of the enemy while simultaneously blocking, trapping and redirecting with the left lead hand. The knife fighter executes an eye or throat slash. While shooting to the enemy's direct right rear, the knife fighter spins 180 degrees while performing an inverted spinning back thrust to the enemy's throat. He then slides his left hand off while grasping the collar and shoulder of the enemy. He jerks back while sweeping the enemy's legs out with his left leg. He then performs a down thrust while covering the body and groin from the knife attack and thrusts into the throat of the enemy.

122

LEFT SPINNING LEG SWEEP

CONTINUED

FIREMEN'S THROW
AGAINST A DOWN THRUST

The knife fighter takes a rear knife fighting position, ready to counterattack with the lead leg checking and kicking, also giving easy maneuverability to either side of the attacker. Remaining light on his lead foot, the knife fighter is able to side-step his adversary. The knife attacker stands in a front knife-fighting position, with the rear foot raised slightly so that he is able to explode as a fencer into his opponent. As the knife attacker steps forward and thrusts down, the knife fighter side-steps to the enemy's left rear with his right lead leg. While simultaneously blocking, trapping and redirecting the knife of the enemy, he thrusts his right hand in front of his body and executes an inverted knife slash on the interior portion of the enemy's wrist. Note at this point that the knife fighter could possibly receive a wound from the enemy's attacking blade, but the knife fighter attacks the inside portion of the enemy's wrist while the enemy is only able to attack the bony exteriors of the knife fighter's left arm. The knife fighter then pulls the enemy's arm towards his left rear, while shifting his weight onto his left leg and rais-ing the right foot up and inside the legs of the enemy. While continuing to pull and redirect the enemy's movements, the knife fighter shoots into a deep squat position while per-forming a groin thrust. The knife fighter pulls, lifts and redirects the enemy's bodyweight onto his back. While lifting, raising, pulling and thrusting, the knife fighter tears the groin of the enemy and throws him directly over his back. Maintaining wrist control, the knife fighter exe-cutes an inside wrist lock while shooting to the enemy's direct right. He rotates, locks and breaks the el-bow across his knee as he drops into a squatting position with his left leg extended and his left knee raised. The knife fighter then executes a powerful down thrust into the enemy's subclavian. Note the thrust of the blade is executed with the en-tire body and driven from the shoul-der, not a mere thrust of the arm.

CONTINUED

CONTINUED

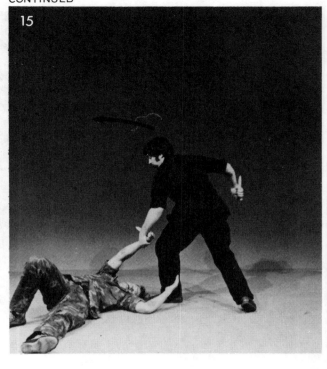

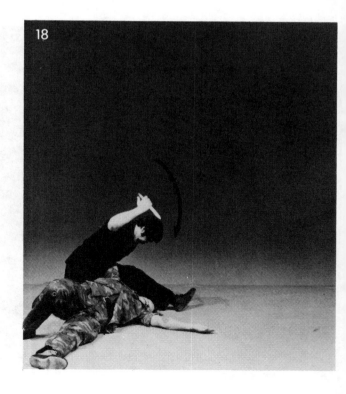

FIREMEN'S THROW
AGAINST A DOWN THRUST

The knife fighter assumes a back fighting stance. He then sidesteps to his direct right while simultaneously blocking, trapping and redirecting the down thrust of the enemy. The knife fighter executes an inverted arm slash while simultaneously pulling and redirecting the weight of the enemy towards his left rear. He executes a groin thrust while performing a firemen's throw.

CONTINUED

COUNTER AGAINST A CROSS-HAND WRIST GRASP

The knife fighter stands in a ready stance with a lead hand reverse hold of the weapon. The enemy jumps forward, grasping the right wrist of the knife fighter with his right hand. The knife fighter then lifts up and traps the hand of the enemy with his left hand while circling in a clock-

138

wise motion over the top of the wrist of the attacker. As he steps back with his right foot, he pulls the enemy to his direct right rear and slashes the wrist while executing a cross-hand wrist lock. He then performs a thrusting instep kick to the groin of the enemy.

COUNTER AGAINST A STRAIGHT-HAND WRIST GRASP

The knife fighter assumes a back fighting stance with a lead hand reverse hold of the weapon. The enemy leaps forward, grasping the right wrist of the knife fighter with his left hand. The knife fighter then thrusts down and forward while stopping the hand of the attacker. He executes a half-circular motion in a counter-clockwise movement. Pulling down, he slashes the wrist and executes a cross-hand wrist lock. He then leaps forward, thrusting his left knee into the enemy's face.

THE MASTER'S THEORY OF MOVEMENT AND COUNTERATTACK

EIGHT POINTS OF THE CIRCLE

The knife fighter evades a fencer's thrust to the eyes by ducking directly down to the immediate right rear of the attacker. He then slashes the stomach, spins 360 degrees to the enemy's right rear, using a spinning back slash, and a circular right-hand thrust to the enemy's right side. The knife fighter then shoots to the enemy's direct rear, driving a powerful knee into the enemy's right thigh, spinning 360 degrees and, double-knife-ripping his back, he spins 360 degrees again to the enemy's direct left, sweeping the enemy's back leg out with a powerful shin kick and leg sweep, returning to a ready position facing a new opponent. This movement should be performed in accordance with the tempo and rhythm of the enemy's movements and reactions. Evade, sidestep and disappear to the enemy's side and rear, sweeping, slashing and evading in preparation for another attack.

Note: This sequence of photos does not represent actual combat knife fighting, but is merely a demonstration of this type of strategy and movement and is intended for use as a demonstrational·training aid only.

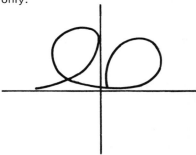

The knife fighter can assume any position, standing relaxed or crouched and prepared for attack. He
(Cont'd.)

CONTINUED

(Cont'd.)

initiates or evades attack by sidestepping to the direct left or right of the enemy's assault, while blocking, trapping and redirecting. Slashing, sweeping and low-kicking, the knife fighter shoots to the immediate side of the enemy, spinning 360 degrees and following up with an exploding kicking, knife-fighting attack or spinning 360 degrees to the immediate rear or opposite side of the enemy, trapping the lead and redirecting it in a circular motion while slashing the neck and sweeping or reaping the legs in a powerful spinning throw. The combat knife fighter is trained always to follow up to a minimum of three vital areas.

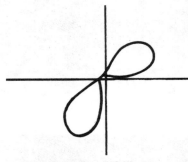

This method of 360-degree spins, in conjunction with sidestepping and evasive movement to the direct rear of the assailant, induces mental disorientation to the attack as the knife

(Cont'd.)

CONTINUED

(Cont'd.)

fighter creates an elusive phantom. He first appears in front of the enemy, then at his side, immediately disappearing to his rear as the enemy has been spun, toppled and thrown to the ground.

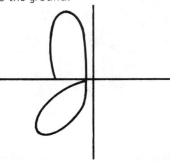

The knife fighter evades, immobilizes and incapacitates the enemy while remaining on his feet. He is physically and mentally prepared for a possible secondary or multiple-man attack. If one or more assailants are encountered, then one must choose the most readily available target. Then attack and redirect the enemy's body into the oncoming path of his fellow assailants, causing momentary delay and confusion. This gives the knife fighter a chance to focus on his point of contact and the ability to calculate his 360-degree, sidestepping, spinning movement in a manner to evade the center of the enemy's attack.

The same method of footwork can be utilized in singular, forward and backward attack and counterattack, or in direct sidestepping, using a singular attack. Double and triple spinning are used during a multiple-man attack, giving the knife fighter the advantage of constant evasive movement.

The master knife fighter is expected to interpret intuitively the attacks of one or multiple men, and to be able to react quickly and decisively to the actions and reactions of the enemy during attack. He must maintain a constant awareness of the eight angles of attack and his method of circular evasion as a direct and lethal escape.

Refer to "A Master's Theory of Strategy and Movement"—Page # 38.

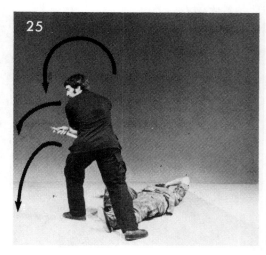

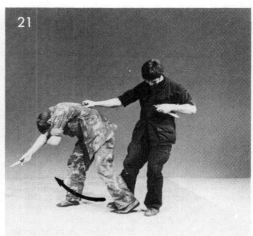

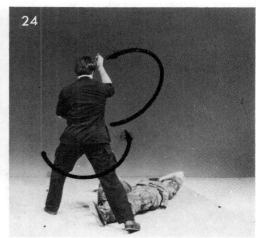

NECK SLASH

Grasping the opponent from the rear, the knife fighter clasps the mouth, leaning the head to the side and rear. This exposes the jugular vein and carotid artery.

He executes an inverted double neck slash at a 45-degree angle.

The fighter then tears the head to the left rear and executes an inverted ripping motion in a straight line through the voice box.

He uses full economy of motion for the purpose of a silent kill.

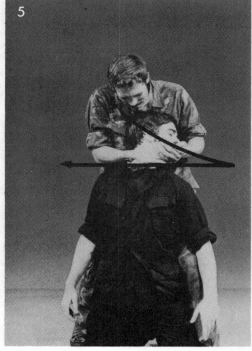

148

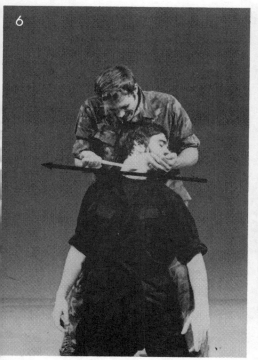

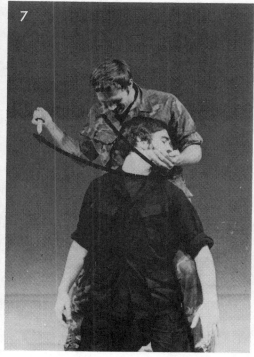

Part II

KNIFE THROWING FOR COMBAT

KNIFE THROWING FOR COMBAT

This section of training should have been entitled "throwing for combat," for the art of throwing, (pyo chang sul pup), encompasses any weapon or object that can be utilized during an attack or counterattack. Throwing one's weapon at his assailant during close-quarter combat can be costly considering the chance of missing, but even greater is the loss of the weapon in case of a secondary attack by multiple attackers. Taking into consideration that during knife throwing, the thrower must maintain a certain pace or interval, (high choke or low choke on the grip of the blade, thus dropping the chances of engaging the enemy and maintaining that interval for a one-to-three second time period consistantly), greatly decreases the justification for throwing the weapon.

Weather factors, rough or unstable terrain, in conjunction with bad mental focus and improper breathing, can all cause the knife fighter to lose that essential edge during combat, to insure the death of the enemy.

The throwing of objects or weapons as a diversionary tactic, or the lead attack of a two-weapon or multiple-weapon attack, causes a delay and effort to evade or block, exposing vital targets of opportunity for the powerful, secondary attack. Double-knife fighting is an example of this method of attack. For instance, during the attack, the knife fighter explodes into the enemy, throwing the lead hand knife or the back hand knife, releasing it at the last moment during the charge, causing the enemy to cover up or evade the attack, and delay for a split second in his attack or counterattack, thus creating that moment that the knife fighter needs during interval change to switch from outside knife fighting

151

to inside knife fighting, the powerful killing zone. The knife is normally thrown at a three to 12-feet interval from the enemy, easily measured by the naked eye, maintaining a minimum of three feet from the target and a maximum of 12 feet. Measure the enemy's distance by using the body height, for as men become smaller, the target decreases in contact area; therefore, it is advisable to adjust interval according to the height of the enemy during combat throwing. For if this is your last alternative, you must take all factors into consideration to insure your survival.

Interval in straight-blade knife throwing is based upon pace, choke on the blade, physical power of the thrower and breathing in conjunction with mental focus; inserting into the target only if all the above coincide with the revolutions of the blade during the throw. Falling into this category of throwing weapons are dirks, daggers and straight-blade throwing knives. Stars, double-bladed throwing knives and any other objects, including rocks, fall into another category of throwing for combat.

During knife throwing, both hands are utilized for generating power and masking the movement of the knife-throwing hand. Creating confusion in the enemy's mind, the knife fighter creates a deceptive attack as he flashes the palm of his nonthrowing hand toward the eyes of the attacker during the cocking and releasing of his hidden knife hand. Much as a magician uses sleight-of-hand to mesmerize and confuse, misdirecting the eyes and minds of the audience, the knife thrower spins, flashes and throws, using body movement and lead-hand-movement as deception. Generating power much like a baseball pitcher, the knife thrower utilizes his entire body, driving all his power from the tip of his toes, through the center of his body. He gives a twisting, thrusting action with his hips, extending his power in a whipping, snapping motion through his shoulder and out the index fingertip of the throwing hand, into the weapon or projectile, maintained during flight until contact.

Breathing is the essence of all power; it is brought into the body by inhaling and extended through and out of the body by exhaling. Its movement is controlled by thought. On right-handed people, the chi or energy enters the body on the left side and is directed out the right side. The opposite applies to left-handed people. Those who are ambidextrous have learned to control both sides equally, normally through mental discipline and can direct the power in either direction with equal force and control. Men tend to favor right or left-handed positions according to their nature, so it is important to train with the concept of equal use by both hands during throwing or knife fighting, for if one arm becomes injured, the other may be utilized.

During the preparation for the throw, the knife fighter must stabilize his breathing so as to create a physical and mental calm. He remains calm, much as a baseball pitcher stands calm just before the windup and throw. Closing the mouth slightly with the tip of the tongue touching the roof of the mouth, he inhales deeply through the nose and forces the air down into the center of the body. The majority of people use only one-third of their normal lung capacity and by focusing off of shallow breathing and into deep breathing, we increase our stamina and endurance tremendously. For those short explosions of power and for the extension of it outside of our bodies, it is essential. Forceful inhaling and holding, in conjunction with forceful exhaling in unison with physical movement creates the rhythm of breathing and body movement for which we are searching.

Visual Images — Mind Control

The key to this entire process is the mental control and visual image maintained throughout the movement. During the initial preparation, the mind calms and clears as the body calms and clears. The knife thrower clears his mind of indecision and negativism. Focusing upon his lower abdomen and breathing, he then visualizes within his mind and feels his total surrounding environment, with his entire body as the baseball pitcher does when he prepares for his throw and there's a man on first base. Even with his back to the runner, the pitcher sees and feels the runner's movement behind him. The knife thrower, then, mentally computes the angles of attack and retreat and visualizes the point of contact, with tremendous mental focus. During combat, the knife fighter must envision things which are close as if they are distant, and things or distinct points which are distant as if they are close at nand. In hwarangdo, we are trained to stare at a small object such as a coin or leaf, and maintain focus upon the minute details. Eventually, as you look deeply and maintain visual focus upon the small detail, the entire object's perspective will change, seemingly making the target appear much larger.

In the novel *SHOGUN*, Buntaro, a Samurai General, shoots three arrows into the night through the thin paper walls of a Japanese Tea House, and as quickly as he fired them, they were embedded, one directly above the other, into a wooden post. The Samurai General, Buntaro, without looking and without thinking, but through pure instinct and intuition, drove the arrows deep within his envisioned target.

Hwarang warriors could ride a horse full out and while passing a target, turn their heads the opposite direction and hit their target dead center. Visualizing the target within the mind and having that distinct positive feeling, 100 percent positive focus and total emotional content towards the completion of the objective, can lead us to this uncanny ability of a dead center hit deep from the center of the man's will. His entire being is projected into the weapon and point of contact. The weapon becomes an extension of the body and mind while in hand, and after release until final contact is made. As a quarterback drops back into the pocket to throw, he sees his target moving. As he releases the ball, he maintains visual contact and follows through toward the movement of the receiver until contact is made. Equally the knife thrower must maintain focus upon the target at hand but he must also be ready to react to a 360-degree possibility of attack, clearing his mind and preparing for another attack or following up on the enemy during his initial throwing attack.

There are 12 different methods of throwing the knife at eight different angles. Training is oriented toward throwing any and all things from these 12 basic methods. Here we will demonstrate some of the integral throwing methods and some of the advanced techniques. Body balance, breath control, focus of mind and extension of chi are the primary factors of success. To insure the highest percentage of consistent strikes and insertions, the knife thrower must consistently practice until the motion becomes second nature, no longer a forced thought and mechanical physical reaction, but a conditioned reflex, an automatic reaction to the adversaries' movements and exposure to vital targets of opportunity.

The knife thrower no longer thinks to throw, but reacts to the situation from his deepest inner nature, developed and perfected after hundreds of thousands of throws. Only after endless hours of practice can we begin to touch the mastery of this combat art.

Remember always that throwing for combat is anything which is readily available and can be utilized as an instrument integral to your survival. The ancient spies of hwarangdo, referred to as "Sul Sa," studied the art of throwing for close-quarter attacks in hallways and doorways, utilizing left-handed and right-handed throws; the agent would throw at the enemy sentries while concealed behind a door or around a corner. They were equally trained while knife fighting in open areas, falling, spinning, jumping and evading, throwing knives as they moved.

Warriors were trained to carry multiple fighting knives and throwing weapons, carrying the knives in every imaginable place. The easy availability to concealment makes the knife an excellent weapon for silent interdictions,. carried behind the collar, up the sleeve of the arm, shoulder holstered inside the jacket along the belt line at the waist, taped or strapped to the legs or hidden in the boots, the knife can be a strong backup if captured, or during the process of escape and evasion.

Star throwing is one of the easiest and most logical methods of throwing, based upon the fact that interval has no bearing, but focus upon spin of the blade during flight, to insure insertion, does. Stars have been used primarily as maiming, delaying weapons, utilized in conjunction with the element of surprise or as a forceful counterattack. Dogs have presented one of the greatest adversaries to experts of infiltration/exfiltration of enemy base camps and high security areas since the art began. The process of evasion is to avoid the dogs or to burn out the dogs' smelling sense with powdered gases and poisons. But if alerted and attacked at close-quarter or tracked by a team of trackers and dogs, the knife and star, or throwing implement, such as a rock, given the correct spin and power, will either kill or decisively delay the attack of the animal, and will be relatively silent compared to the report of a handgun or rifle.

Guard dogs will normally take the arm or the leg for control purposes and they are easily detoured because they tend to stay at arm's or leg's length. But attack dogs shoot for the neck and groin and are programmed to maim or kill. These animals should be met in a low, powerful and well-guarded position with the lead leg protecting the groin and the lead forearm and elbow protecting the body and throat. The back hand should conceal the weapon and protect it from being dislodged during the attack. The attacking dog may be met with a powerful throw of the knife when the animal reaches a three-to-six foot interval from the defender; and the same should be considered for the onslaught of an enemy soldier. From the low crouch position, one can throw the weapon, then dive and roll to either side of the attack, evading and preparing for his next counterattack. This method is used only if you have multiple weapons or as a last chance for delay or evasion.

If the weapon is your only advantage and you have access to nothing else, then you must absorb the attack and attempt to redirect the forward momentum after the initial shock, to the right or left, attacking the adversary with *a fierceness* one-thousand-fold of the attacker, for in hand-to-hand combat, the soldier has but two choices—*Win or Die!* So never throw away the strongest advantage you have, on a one-shot chance of survival. Evade, and attack while retreating and you will have led the adversary into your trap, for the master attack is the counterattack.

ROCK THROWING

Rock throwing is as old as primeval man. Stonings were religious punishment in Biblical times; David killed Goliath by slinging a rock. Polynesian warriors killed wild boar and attacking enemy while many North American Indians survived because of their ability to kill small game by throwing sharpened stones.

Hwarang warriors and other Asian warriors of medieval times studied the art of throwing stones. Many of the roads and highways were of cobblestone or had small stones, rubbed flat and smooth by the constant travel of the path, creating an edge and their roundness, giving them a symmetrical form similar to a throwing star or a frisbee of today. With a snapping motion of the arm and flipping motion of the wrist, the projectile begins to spin in flight, producing a cutting effect as it strikes, being much more powerful than the nonrevolutionary, straight throw, due to the fact that two forces are at play: the forward momentum of the projectile and the centrifugal force, created by the spin given by the thrower's whipping action as he throws with his entire body.

The present day Grand Master of hwarangdo, Joo Bang Lee, was taught by his master, Saum Dosa, who could take small hardened nuts and throw them, embedding them deeply within the wood of trees.

Special breathing is for the development of power and tremendous concentration, such as when a person is very frightened and demonstrates superhuman feats of strength or speed, lifting a vehicle off an injured friend after an accident to free him, or moving from one point to another so quickly during a firefight that no one hits him. This type of mental/physical power directed with tremendous concentration to vital areas can make even the smallest, most insignificant piece of our surrounding a lethal, self-protecting weapon. Many times psychologists suggest that the color red is associated with aggression and anger. In hwarangdo, we are taught to visualize upon the color intonation red during battle and deep concentration, along with the specific point of contact and actually visualizing and feeling the impact and reaction—rather a mental/physical follow-through. Combined with 100 percent emotional content for the completion of the objective, we can possibly extract this latent power of the body and mind at will and direct it through physical movement and concentration of thought.

Many a straw has been found embedded deeply within a tree or telephone pole after the tremendous onslaught of a hurricane. Here, as the body and mind of the thrower merge, the force and power of the hurricane are exemplified as he spins and throws. His precision and accuracy are exemplified as even the smallest objects may become deadly objects of self-protection, much as the straw embedded within the tree during a hurricane. Only through tremendous concentration can we achieve such power, but man is mind and we are limited only by thought. Ingenuity and positive thinking are the keys to the mind, *and to your survival in combat.*

Michael D. Echanis

DIRECT OVERHAND THROW

The knife thrower stands physically relaxed and mentally calm in preparation for the throw. While inhaling deeply from the lower abdomen, he steps forward with his left foot, raising his left forearm and hand in front of the body while adjusting 80 percent of his weight to the rear leg. Then with a cocking motion similar to a quarterback throwing a football, he cocks his right arm directly behind his head in preparation for the delivery of the throw. The knife thrower then flashes his left palm forward in a rising, dropping, circular motion towards the enemy, flashing the palm of the lead hand towards the enemy's eyes, utilizing the movements as a diversionary tactic. Then with a whipping, snapping motion of the wrist, arm and shoulder, in conjunction with a powerful thrusting motion of the hips, he directs all his power from the base of his toes through the center of his body. Directed by the extension of the index finger of the throwing hand, the knife fighter then drives all his weight and power from the tip of his toes and from the very ground itself, through his body out the extended arm and into the weapon, forcefully exhaling with the release of the weapon. The knife thrower must maintain a distinct visual image of the target within his mind. This is the easiest and most direct type of overhand throw to use. Keep in mind that the movements of these techniques are done in practice form and each movement must be readjusted to real combat situations, utilizing the fastest, most powerful, direct attack possible. These movements are practiced to develop speed, form, power and mental focus to be utilized in conjunction with breath control. The most logical method of throwing any weapon is the method that fits your needs, psychologically and physically, and conforms to the situation at hand.

DIRECT SIDE ARM THROW

The knife thrower shoots directly forward while simultaneously cocking the right arm and protecting the body with the lead left hand. He then delivers the throw in a side-arm movement, much like a baseball pitcher delivers a submarine pitch. If a star is thrown, it is delivered with a snapping, whipping motion, causing it to spin in flight, similar to skipping a rock across water. The projectile builds speed and power through centrifugal force as it spins in flight. All throwing techniques are for practical use with any object. The thrower himself must adjust his grip or choke, delivery of the knife, spin of the weapon to the feel, weight, distribution and geometrical proportions of the weapon utilized.

161

WHIPPING OVERHAND THROW

The knife thrower stands calm and relaxed, visualizing the target at hand. He then steps forward with his left leg, simultaneously raising the left hand and arm in front of the body, concealing the movement of the knife hand and delivering the weapon in a half-moon, circular motion towards the enemy. Never really cocking the throwing hand, he delivers the weapon with a whipping 180-degree circular motion, driving his entire bodyweight and power forward in rhythm with the throw. Driving the power of the throw from his toes to his fingertips, the thrower directs an action of the follow-through with the extension of the index finger of the throwing hand. This type of movement utilizes the generation of power through total body rhythm in conjunction with circular whipping of the arms and upper body. Since the motions delay the time of the delivery, 'the movements must be concealed by the body, the eyes and mind of the enemy, distracted and diverted by the movements of the empty hand, in a rhythmic, hypnotic manner, then followed by an explosive, shocking throw of the weapon directly to an exposed vital area.

162

WHIPPING UNDERHAND THROW

The knife thrower stands relaxed, grasping the butt of the weapon. Stepping forward with the left leg while simultaneously concealing the movement of the knife hand, bringing the left hand in a raising, circular motion in front of the body, the knife thrower whips his knife hand forward, using the movement of his left hand as a deceptive diversionary tactic. The knife thrower whips the knife in a 360-degree circular motion in an underhand motion towards the enemy. As the weapon is delivered in an underhand thrusting motion, the palm of the left hand is flashed above the head of the knife thrower, distracting the enemy's eyes from the true delivery of the weapon.

164

180-DEGREE LEFT
BACK SPINNING THROW

The knife thrower simulates a rear attack mentally. He spins 180 degrees to his direct left and rear. Utilizing his lead hand as a diversionary tactic, the knife thrower follows up by releasing the knife with the second hand in a powerful follow-through.

166

180-DEGREE RIGHT
BACK SPINNING THROW

The knife thrower spins 180 degrees to his direct right rear, throwing the knife with his lead hand in a thrusting back hand motion. He focuses on the point of contact and directs his flow of power through the extended index finger and body into the weapon and target itself.

SHOULDER HOLSTER THROW

The knife thrower delivers the weapon from a waistband, wrist-band or shoulder holster. Feinting forward with his left hand and raising his lead right leg, the knife thrower leaps forward, flashing the palm of his empty hand toward the eyes of the enemy and delivers the weapon in a direct thrusting motion with the throwing hand. This technique uses a throw similar to the type utilized at a three-to-six-foot interval. The weapon, if not multipointed and containing straight-like features, should be thrown in a direct thrusting motion, avoiding any revolutions of the blade while in flight. This technique is excellent for close-quarters use in buildings and alleyways.

DROPPING SPIN BACK THROW

The knife thrower, utilizing the element of surprise, cross-steps to his direct right front, with his left hand simultaneously pointing and directing the eyes of the enemy to the right and concealing the movements of the knife hand with his body during movement. The knife can be pulled from the right leg position, a waistband, a shoulder holster, the sleeve or collar clasp. Using a deceptive movement and element of surprise, he then spins 360 degrees to his right while simultaneously dropping to avoid being hit by counterattack and delivering the weapon in a direct back hand thrusting motion. This is a graceful movement and can be deceptively effective.

DIRECT UNDERHAND THROW

The knife fighter conceals the weapon while stepping forward with his left lead leg. The knife thrower whips the weapon directly underhand in a thrusting motion, utilized in conjunction with the thrusting movements of the hips and body. The knife thrower delivers the throw at a three-to-six-foot interval from the enemy. This is a very fast and direct manner of throwing any weapon and is normally done without any spin or rotation to the projectile.

175

180-DEGREE BACK SPINNING THROW

The knife thrower stands with his back to the enemy. He then spins 180 degrees to his right rear and delivers the weapon in a whipping, snapping motion, driving the entire motion of his body forward towards the enemy as he throws. This technique is utilized for the element of surprise and for counterattack from rear attack.

360-DEGREE SPINNING THROW

The knife thrower generates power and causes deception as he spins 360 degrees to his left rear, building power and force as he spins and whips towards the enemy, using the lead hand as a deceptive distraction and simultaneously protecting the body as he spins, turns and throws. This type of motion is utilized to develop speed and power while causing deception and giving the knife thrower a 360-degree awareness of his surroundings. Many times this throw is utilized while surrounded by multiple attackers.

DIVING ROLLING
OVERHAND THROW
(WITH KNIFE)

The knife thrower, to avoid attack or counterattack, charges the enemy and dives forward so as to change target exposure and interval from the enemy and to deceive the enemy of the movement of his knife throwing hand. The knife thrower then dives to his left front or right front and springs forward as he makes a 360-degree turn, delivering the weapon with an overhand, whipping motion, coming back to a standing position upon delivery, focusing the power of the roll from the movement itself through the body and into the projectile.

180

DIVING ROLLING OVERHAND THROW (WITH SHURIKEN)

The knife thrower, to avoid attack or counterattack, charges the enemy and dives forward so as to change target exposure and interval from the enemy and to deceive the enemy of the movement of his knife throwing hand. The knife thrower then dives to his left front or right front and springs forward as he makes a 360-degree turn, delivering the weapon with an overhand, whipping motion, coming back to a standing position upon delivery, focusing the power of the roll from the movement itself through the body and into the projectile.

RETRIEVING THE WEAPON

It is possible that during combat the soldier may drop his weapon or he may find himself without his weapon and the only weapon readily available is upon the ground. The knife thrower must continue to move for fear of becoming a stationary target and he finds the need to dive and roll, scooping the weapon up as he performs a forward roll and springing forward into a standing position for the delivery of the weapon. In practice, one must focus his eyes upon the weapon during the forward roll while still maintaining an awareness of his total surroundings and the enemy at hand.

FOOT SCOOPING ROCK THROW

The knife thrower steps forward with his right foot, scooping up the rock with the arch of his foot. Shooting the left hand down and simultaneously grasping the rock, the knife thrower flips the rock to his right hand while concealing his movement with the turning of his body and spinning 360 degrees towards the enemy and to the knife thrower's left rear. The knife thrower then whips his left hand forward towards the enemy, causing him to believe the weapon is to be delivered by the lead hand. With the enemy unaware of the exchange during movement, the knife thrower then delivers the weapon with an overhand whipping motion.

CONCLUSION

In the study of unconventional warfare, the paramilitary operative is expected to remain and survive for extended periods of time behind enemy lines, sometimes isolated and alone. The discipline and psychological stability required to outstay the enemy for extended periods of time in his own environment can be developed and maintained only after countless hours of training and a lifelong commitment to self-discipline; not the mass-produced item of the divisional training camps, but the individually selected soldier who is willing to devote his life to the elite of the professional soldiers.

There is no substitute for the most expensive commodity of them all—progressive combat-oriented training, leading to a well-trained combat-oriented soldier. By progressive we mean the constant individual and team progression towards excellence, as each training session leads each individual member closer to perfect timing and reaction and we begin to create a fine-tuned fighting machine. We are only as strong as the weakest man within our team; therefore, it is the responsibility of the individual soldier to test himself constantly and strive for perfection. The very essence of special warfare training should be orientation towards the psychological/physical combat-readiness of the individual soldier, not the battalions on paper but highly trained, highly motivated, individual professional soldiers working together as a team.

Please bear in mind that the study of hand-to-hand combat has been used as the basis of discipline in the training of warriors since the warrior class was created.

Hand-to-hand combat can be utilized as a form of self-improvement, a competitive sport or as an educational system, but never losing the context of its objective and, therefore, training is always executed in its combat form. It can be a means of utilizing the most basic physical training programs and directing them towards combat-readiness, giving the individual soldier a needed change of routine and instilling a sense of self-confidence through increased physical ability and mental alertness, leading to a true fighting spirit.

In the elite Special Warfare units of the military, it is essential that every individual soldier be in a state of 24-hour combat-readiness; therefore, he must maintain the highest physical and mental standards of excellence. Only through a lifelong dedication to a way of life and a form of discipline can one expect to achieve these high standards of professionalism. For every man who enters the elite with the ideal of being the best, these goals and standards must apply.

Hopefully, the study conducted by this Research Group has led us to an effective system for the development of programs to instill these virtues. This is the first basic study on this subject matter and by no means does this imply that it is a complete study of the psychological/physical results of hand-to-hand combat training and its effects on the individual soldier and its relationship to the overall combat-readiness of the Special Warfare units concerned, but only as a basis of understanding, so that every man who reads this book may search within himself to discover, through his own ingenuity and creative ability, techniques that will adapt to the situation and conform to his psychological/physical needs.

Future volumes will deal with advanced fighting systems, oriented towards the mastery of the knife and other weapons as needed for combat use.

STUDY GROUP A
Office of Research & Development
Director of Psycho-Physical Studies

—Michael D. Echanis

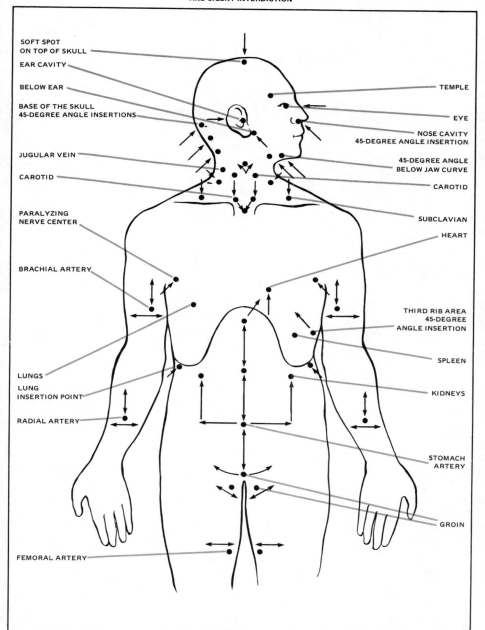

SOFT SPOT
ON TOP OF SKULL

EAR CAVITY

BELOW EAR

BASE OF THE SKULL
45-DEGREE ANGLE INSERTIONS

JUGULAR VEIN

CAROTID

PARALYZING
NERVE CENTER

BRACHIAL ARTERY

LUNGS

LUNG
INSERTION POINT

RADIAL ARTERY

FEMORAL ARTERY

TEMPLE

EYE

NOSE CAVITY
45-DEGREE ANGLE INSERTION

45-DEGREE ANGLE
BELOW JAW CURVE

CAROTID

SUBCLAVIAN

HEART

THIRD RIB AREA
45-DEGREE
ANGLE INSERTION

SPLEEN

KIDNEYS

STOMACH
ARTERY

GROIN

*Arrows show angle of knife insertion and areas considered vital during a slashing attack. Primarily 45-degree angle cuts are utilized in the use of any cutting-edged weapon.

*The most important factor in the use of a knife, is focused attack, slashes and stabs directed at vital areas as targets of opportunity appear in the enemy's defense. Bear in mind the length of the blade in proportion to the depth of the artery or vein during knife insertion.